The NEW MUSIC

The NEW MUSIC
By GEORGE DYSON

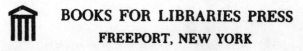

BOOKS FOR LIBRARIES PRESS

FREEPORT, NEW YORK

First Published 1924
Reprinted 1970

STANDARD BOOK NUMBER:

8369-5231-6

LIBRARY OF CONGRESS CATALOG CARD NUMBER:

72-109622

PRINTED IN THE UNITED STATES OF AMERICA

NOTE

MOST of the material in this book has been used in lectures given under circumstances where substantial musical illustrations could also be employed. Fragmentary musical quotations inevitably suffer by lack of context, but it is hoped that the reader's experience will enable him to remedy this defect.

I am indebted to Mr. A. H. Fox Strangways, Editor of *Music and Letters*, for the serial publication of the chapters on Texture in that journal, and for his permission to reprint them here.

G. D.

November 1923.

CONTENTS

THE NEW MUSIC

QUESTIONS OF PERSPECTIVE

Cannot a man live free and easy
Without admiring Pergolesi,
Or through the world in comfort go
That never heard of Doctor Blow ? . . .
I would not go four miles to visit
Sebastian Bach (or Batch, which is it ?) . . .
*Charles Lamb : ' Free Thoughts on some Eminent
Composers '.*

The reason why my brother's so severe,
Vincentio, is—my brother has no ear ; . . .
His spite at music is a pretty whim.
He loves not it, because it loves not him.
Mary Lamb to Vincent Novello.

THERE is perhaps no adventure in artistic
criticism so rash as the attempt to describe a
contemporary revolution. At such a time
every novelty is essentially experimental. Apart from
a general, and not infrequently a somewhat feverish,
impatience with tradition, there may be no conclusive
evidence of such common aims and ideals as might
give the movement a clear direction and purpose. It
is dangerous to assume that even the most convincing
of the immediate products of reform have more than
temporary significance. The speculations of enthusiasm may be founded on very fragmentary grounds.
It is, moreover, the natural privilege of each succeed-
ing generation to point out how blindly its fathers
have erred, and in the historical perspective of criticism there is no feature more striking than the high
confidence with which men have uttered prophetic
blunders. Strong views, whether of praise or blame,

B

seem so often to attach themselves to matters of little ultimate importance. The very selection of events on which the critic chooses to exercise his faculties may betray an attitude of mind which is fatal to the permanence of his values. It is just this prevailing attitude towards a given problem which changes so frequently and so profoundly, and the inquirer who is conscious of the quicksand upon which all his judgements may be built must either bridle his tongue or court the derision of his successors. Towards contemporary movements he can, broadly speaking, react in but one of two ways. He can be non-committal, or he can be overbold. The former procedure is of small practical use to anyone. The latter may deliver him a hostage to posterity. And it is interesting to remark how such contrasts of temper have alternated in history. A generation which expresses itself strongly is normally followed by one which prefers to be more wary. Scepticism is the child of prophecy.

That the twentieth century is not in love with forcible expositions of belief will hardly be disputed. The perfectibility of societies and institutions is no longer an axiom of thought. What is sometimes called the illusion of progress seems more accurately to describe contemporary experience. Progress no longer resembles a road along which events may be said to march. The evolution of ideas, and of the actions to which they give rise, is now more aptly comparable to the structure of a tree whose many branches appear to issue fortuitously. Some will spread farther or rise higher than others, but of none can it be held that it will never be superseded or surpassed. The whole organisation is inherently competitive, and once the various parts are differentiated, they can never again coalesce. Even the best and most powerful of them will eventually cease to be fertile, and it is often necessary to begin again very humbly in order to build hopefully anew. Thus the original mind, in philosophy and art alike, often seeks a more primitive, a more fundamental point of view from which to fashion its theories of thought and action, and the only connection between rival principles may be deeply hidden in the soil of experience. All particular developments outlive their usefulness. There comes a moment which, for a given system, is final. The structure may die gradually, or it may crash to its end. In either event a new beginning has to be made, for the foundations of which a wise architect will endeavour to dig deeper than before.

Every period has its confused and conflicting ideals, its innumerable examples of growth and decay, and a strong-minded generation takes pride in a party spirit. It will roundly condemn, or frankly extol, as the case may be. Half measures will be intolerable to it. The character of our present age is decidedly not of this type. Intolerance is out of fashion. We suffer, more or less politely, crudities or extravagances which we no more genuinely admire than did our fathers who thundered against them. We are obsessed by the recollection that this same thunder was so frequently misapplied. It was a two-edged weapon which did not encourage detailed discrimination. It was, from our more detached point of view, far too clumsy and far too autocratic. We prefer to be circumspect, and in the practice of circumspection it is tempting to hold the view that the search for permanent standards of value is hopeless.

It is true that standards of judgement will change. Criticism can be no more static than the experience on which it is founded. But to exalt this truism into a negation is to be sceptical to the verge of paralysis. The expressed creed of an artistic faith will have as many variants as there are minds which reflect on it, and the more striking innovations of a would-be reformer are as likely to be forgotten heresies as new truths. But artistic faith itself, quite apart from the form in which it may be clothed, is one of the prime

3

values of experience, and truth is often translated into action by virtue of the battles that are waged around it. We of this age have dwelt too much on what we are pleased to consider the artistic stupidity of the men who fought Wagner, or Ibsen, or some other apostle of reform. We have forgotten that there were ideals on both sides, and ideals for which a good deal could be said. It is at least better to have a philosophy of mere conservation than to cherish no active ideas at all. The most exasperating opponents of reform did at least believe in something which to them was worth fighting for, and they played a useful part. It is opposition of this kind which purges revolution of its vapouring and extravagance. That half the audience could not sit through our first performance of the Choral Symphony a century ago is a measure of Beethoven's ultimate triumph. His music had to fight for its place. So had the music of Wagner. And if there is one feature which, more than another, might make us view the artistic daring of the twentieth century with misgiving, it is the fact that there is so little bitterness in the fight about it. Any kind of novelty will to-day find a certain number of easy converts, whose exaggerated enthusiasm is no unqualified recommendation. Serious reformers indeed suffer more by the indiscipline of their friends than by the machinations of their enemies. The tribute of a powerful and coherent opposition is not often granted to the contemporary iconoclast. A few of the old school still fulminate in private, but that public which used to be either frankly hostile or intelligently converted seems to have vanished. Feeble deprecation is balanced by faint praise.

It will be sufficient to give one example of how this lack of critical faith can affect contemporary art, encouraging the most childish heresies to ape the manners of a new truth. One of the most loudly advertised of the new gospels of recent years is the

4

movement which in many arts has been grouped under the general title of Futurism. So far as the graphic arts as a whole are concerned, Futurism in its sanest mood preached a revolt from representation, from manual photography, from all that is realistic in technique. In pursuit of this ideal it extolled the unique position of music, which has its own peculiar medium in which it can be completely expressed, and which owes little or nothing in the technical sense either to nature or to the imitation of nature. Futurism invited the graphic arts to develop a comparable technique of their own, a technique in which the graphic adventures of lines, spaces, masses, and colours should be themselves the vehicles of an intrinsic beauty, a beauty no more bound to natural objects than is the beauty which music evolves from sound. Theoretically, this is a truly æsthetic ideal. The graphic arts have always found their most intimate forms of expression in those elements which, transformed by the vision and hand of the artist, have thus escaped the mechanism of representation. Decoration essentially involves graphic purity of this kind, and there is no logical reason why an art of painting or an art of sculpture should not flourish which might owe as little to the strict imitation of nature as do the proportions of architecture or the texture of music. But this same futuristic school, when it touched music, became a farrago of nonsense. Its music was to desert just that formal purity which the graphic arts were said to lack, and to indulge in all kinds of infantile realisms, using the complicated apparatus of the orchestra, for example, to manufacture imitative effects of incredible silliness. The futuristic art of the pencil was to be pure design, the futuristic art of music was to be the noise of a farmyard. This is perhaps an extreme instance of æsthetic confusion, but analogous contradictions of principle are to be found in the internal handling of many contemporary artistic problems.

5

Yet there can be no coherent work, either creative or appreciative, without reasoned convictions or stable intuitions of some kind, be they no more than principles of selection. Futurism as a whole was a contradiction in terms.

Inconsistency is the despair of those lovers of an art who are not unsympathetic to reform, for the unravelling of confused issues is a thankless task. Yet loose thinking, if it be unchecked, will always tend to weaken even the most firm lessons of experience. Criticism should be most tireless when reformers are most aggressive. Not only must tradition itself be examined without prejudice, but reform must be made to show, if it can, at least an equal measure of sense. An atmosphere of active discussion is the proper precursor of broader views. Though scepticism is not always in season, it is none the less true that new theories would hardly make headway if there were no flaws in the old. It might have been untimely, for example, to challenge Bach's adoption and fortification of a particular system of intervals of pitch, two centuries ago. In spite of its restricting music to the twelve semitones we know, and thus preventing the possibility of any more delicate distinctions, it did for its time offer obvious advantages. Composers were enabled to explore in one movement all the available keys, and to relate them to one another unambiguously. Yet the pursuit of this practical end has brought music within sight, theoretically, of a blank wall of finality. It was, in its degree, as if painting had decreed that the seven conventional colour divisions of the rainbow should be made exclusive, no intermediate or other tints being permitted in the art. We are now, as will be seen in due course, at much closer grips with this fundamental limitation of our music, and it is no longer possible to ignore the implications which such a convention was sure to raise, sooner or later, in acute form. Similarly it might have appeared perverse, a century ago, to challenge Beethoven's

6

exploitation of dynamic vigour in music. His was a personality great enough to be master of the method, rather than to be mastered by it. But he did undoubtedly encourage that progressive dependence on quantity and vehemence of expression which led the music of the nineteenth century to tolerate many a still cruder form of emotional stimulation. These are but two of the legacies of tradition with which the twentieth century has to deal, and some of its pangs are certainly due to the discomfort caused by inherited restrictions which it is as yet impotent to shake off. No experiment is too wild if it seems to promise freedom. These are the throes which some will identify with birth, some with death. There can be no more urgent problem than their diagnosis.

To cover the whole ground of contemporary novelty is impossible. The inquirer must betray himself by selection and snap his fingers at posterity. Posterity will probably deride his conclusions in any event. So much risk must be faced. But even with regard to what clearly ought to be included, there are great difficulties. Music to-day is an art which in many respects differs fundamentally from the music of earlier times. It has undergone a transformation similar to that which has affected letters. The invention of printing is generally held to be the crucial event in the diffusion of literature, though for a long time after this letters remained comparatively speaking of the few and for the few. It was not until the advent of a more or less universal system of education that the reading public, and hence the literature addressed to it, became the heterogeneous and unwieldy mass it now is. Music is fast reaching this same condition. Its diffusion was fostered by printing, but it was still necessary that there should be specialised readers and performers, and these were few. All the musicians, all the amateurs, and indeed all the regular audiences of Europe a century ago were together but a very small proportion of the public.

7

The art they fostered remained to this extent eclectic, and it was possible for a connoisseur to be fairly in touch with the whole of it. To-day music is as widely diffused as European culture itself. The number of people who read and practise it has augmented largely, but far more important than this is its present alliance with mechanical reproduction. There has arisen in our day a musical public comparable in size with that which supports literary journalism. And there is no barrier of language. Music is now almost a world-speech, and its international circulation is already so highly organised that a work which has been effectively launched in one of the centres of production may be heard within a very short time throughout the whole extent of western civilisation. The remote farm on the Canadian prairies quickly hears and enjoys the music which a London theatre has approved. The music-halls of South America are hardly distinguishable, musically, from those of Moscow or Melbourne, and it is rare to find any place where men of European descent are congregated, without some form of reproduction of a music which is to all intents the same throughout. The taste of the whole world, whether we agree with it or not, now has its foundation in this community of experience. The more qualified music which an older fashion would have considered to be alone worthy of attention has thus to face a new competition, and this brings with it a change of perspective, which to ignore is to risk a considerable distortion of view.

No critic of literature would fail to remember the effect which journalism may have on standards of literary taste. No more must the amateur of music forget that, whatever his own personal bias may be, he is yet to some degree concerned with a stream of experience of which his own is only a microscopic fragment. For one composer of the older type there are now a thousand musical journalists. For one culti-vated listener there are ten thousand who are frankly
8

ingenuous. The selective taste of a cultured few may mean little or nothing to these latter. They demand experience at first hand, they are impatient of authority, and there is no guarantee that their capacity for discrimination is of a high order. It is indeed more likely that as a circle of appreciation widens its quality will suffer. In any case, the only music which is in the first place provided for this aggregated public is such as the journalist in music may be able to supply. It is not his function to write for posterity. He is the purveyor of a talent which is by definition ephemeral. Like his literary colleague, he is essentially anonymous, in that his artistic personality is usually merged in a prevailing fashion. It is enough if he does his work well. It is good fortune if he is able to do it with distinction. His virtues are those of the masses to whom he appeals. He is sentimental, whimsical, pathetic, vulgar, passionate, stirring, or humorous by turns, but always with a bold pen. Those to whom he speaks are busied with action rather than with thought, and art for them must represent an amusement or a distraction which may have very little to do with classical values. The technique of the journalist is to-day remarkably able. Compare the skill with which a popular tune is now harmonically dressed, with the crudities of fifty years ago. Technical vices, and this is a matter of great importance, are almost without exception derived from the classics. The modern English ballad is descended from the facile songs of those on whom the mantle of the classics was supposed to rest. Thence came also the cheapest of our part-songs and anthems, our popular cantatas and services, and the whole category of instrumental drawing-room music. Even the writers of popular dances have done little more than purloin the more obvious mannerisms of the pseudo-classics. These superficial turns of speech are not invented by the journalist. The most commonplace elements in popular music are for the most part

9

exploitations of the weaknesses of those serious composers whose inspiration was thin or whose mannerisms were infectious. And this is the music which is fast becoming the mother's milk on which we are all, at some time or other, forcibly fed. It cannot but affect the demands of the embryonic amateur if and when he aspires to artistic adolescence.

For it is in fact from this background of popular taste that the audiences which support a more serious view of the art are now recruited. The cultured patrons and the effective bodies of intelligent amateurs who enabled the great composers of the past to live and work no longer exist in organised form. They had their limitations and were not always either charitable or enlightened, but they were at least a definable and coherent public to which genius could address itself. To-day the amateurs of music are more numerous, but they come from the most diverse quarters. They have little corporate unity or close tradition. They represent, in the flood of an artistic democracy, disparate elements which are very difficult to focus. While there is no novelty that will not find a certain number of followers, there are many music lovers who with unfailing integrity are seekers of the best. What is perhaps beyond achievement is the definite harnessing of these latter in a way that will make their convictions effective. Too frequently it seems to be only those enthusiasts who can make the most noise who can hope to be heard, and the rank and file are thus led hither and thither by a succession of mutually destructive advertisements. The chances of survival which await works of genuine merit are probably more slender than ever before.

It requires but a slight acquaintance with contemporary work to show how this chaos of opinions affects all but the most adamant of serious artists. There is an unremitting pressure which constrains men of real discrimination to compete with those whose

10

ideals are doubtful or negative. An illuminating example of this process is the way in which we seem to be compelled to edit our classics. A public fed on variegated sweetmeats cannot appreciate the flavour of a more austere fare. Conscious of this, and with a desire to escape its consequences, we ' arrange ' the old masters. We modernise the text, altering the scoring, adding phrasing and marks of expression, accentuating rhythms, and fortifying tunes. We perform the work in a manner as closely as possible akin to the style which happens to be fashionable now, or which suits the technique of a particular type of performer. In extreme cases we virtually steal the prestige of a famous name and attach it to what is largely a new work. Of our good intent there is no doubt. Mozart's additions to Handel were also a work of devotion. But the question of principle remains. We have to play Bach on the modern piano. We can alter Bach to suit the piano of the concert-room, or we can discipline the piano to values as near as possible to those of Bach. It is the same with the old symphonies and suites. We can rewrite them to fit the modern orchestra, or we can reduce our orchestra to proportions that will be true to the original work. There are solid arguments to be advanced on both sides. But what the editors have really in view are the large numbers and varied tastes of the public they desire to convince. The purist, on the other hand, is jealous to preserve those beauties which cannot be broadcast.

The most promising attempt to provide music with an enlightened public now concentrates its attention on education. There is an enormous amount of music written and cultivated not only for its own sake, but also for the effect it is calculated to have in the encouragement of sound taste. There are no easy classics, and much of the teaching which used to be somewhat vainly devoted to the less technically difficult works of the great masters now prefers to attack its objective less directly, while for the training of the listener as such there are admirable mechanical allies. An acknowledged concern with popular taste is also shown in contemporary devotion to folk-music. Folk-music is to provide a link between music that is popular and music that is good. It is in no literal sense music of the twentieth-century folk. It cannot compete in popularity with its modern counterpart. But there is probably in all of us a certain fringe of hereditary memory, a capacity for education in some favoured direction, and it is to this strain that our own folk-music should minister. The difficulties here are of the type already remarked. So far as folk-tunes are unscrupulously arranged and exploited, they may achieve popularity at the expense of the very qualities that are their essential worth. And the same is true of the thousand pieces which are written for educational purposes. Technically they represent a great gain, for degrees of difficulty are now well understood. But the problem of taste remains. When educational music is too austere it does not appeal. When it is too superficial it does not educate.

The love of good music is an acquired taste. Hence come both our difficulties and our hopes. Endowments of sensitiveness are infinitely varied, but however rich they may be, they are in the first place no more than a capacity for experience ; they are not a substitute for it. Experience provides the field in which discrimination is exercised and trained. This is education. We may be conscious only intermittently, if at all, of our processes of growth, and introspection may do little more than register phases. But we do from time to time reach a lively sense of values. We can recall occasions when Wagner, or Beethoven, or Bach grew into a new stature. And just as these clarities enlighten all our experience, so they in turn are subject to the influence of later or more vivid impressions. There can be no appreciation without values, but a living appreciation

12

connotes living values. Standards of taste are real, not in spite of their vagaries, but because of them. What progressive evolution demands is the will to acquire, the desire rigorously to prove.

That sound taste can thus propagate itself is clear in a thousand ways. The story of the Queen's Hall Promenade Concerts is but one of many examples. Even on the lowest ground of sheer popularity, the Fifth Symphony of Beethoven towers above innumerable shallower works. The most universal musical idol that England has ever known is Handel's *Messiah*, one of the major works in all music. Even Bach is at long last coming into his own. This power of the best to endure is the foundation of all rational belief. Given the will to know, no environment is too modest to furnish substantial gains. The village chorus aspires to the *Messiah*. Still more illuminating are the artistic fortunes of that delightfully indigenous institution, the brass band. A score of men in a remote neighbourhood, having apparently no artistic antecedents either individually or collectively, will tackle an array of difficult instruments and, in the intervals of working hard for a living, will make themselves into sound executive musicians. What do they play ? In the first place, dances and marches and popular tunes. These are simple in outline, and are to be had in technically easy forms. But soon the 'selection' is demanded ; from musical comedy, from light opera, from grand opera. From this latter follows inevitably the desire to attempt overtures and suites, including the best. These men acquire taste by pure experience, they reach the classics by natural selection, and it is not long before the only limit to their appreciation may be the catalogue of works available for their particular organization. There is a hierarchy of standards which will capitulate by degrees to any music-lover whose pursuit is keen.

It is when this natural evolution of successive values takes place in the most sensitive of all the elements in music—in the mind, that is, of the creative artist himself—that the task of keeping pace with it may become formidable or impossible. The work of original genius is not likely to fall effortless into traditional categories. The composer's sensitiveness is often almost pathological. The violence of his reactions to heritage and to convention is frequently but an index of his vitality. It is therefore hardly surprising that a period of artistic expansion should display a haste and a complexity in its aims and methods, which no hard and fast analogies will reduce to order. This difficulty of pace has always confronted the contemporary amateur, and to it have been due many of his bewilderments and misgivings. It will disappear only when music has reached its end. And when to these natural uncertainties are added the complications of a democratic patronage, the worship of size, the advertisement of noise, the temptation to amaze rather than to convince, then the old problem of how the true prophet is to make himself understood is aggravated to an acute degree. The greater the worth of a new truth, the less easily will it obey fashions of time and place. And because the prophet is not without honour in theory, whatever may be his unfortunate fate in the flesh, there will always be writers who choose to be astounding, or enigmatic, or incoherent, because in some such disguise, so it appears to them, were the famous oracles of the past enwrapped. Thus a promising talent may be led to underline its extravagances. Thus many a music-lover, asking for wheat, may be given chaff.

The prophet in music is the composer. His evangelist is the performer. This partnership is akin to that of the drama, and the influence which actors and managers have on the prevailing taste of the theatre is exactly paralleled by the power of the executive musician to affect the fortunes of music. Performers would be more than human if they were able completely to dissolve their own ideals and ambitions in the thoughts of

14

another mind. Under normal circumstances they would not even succeed as exponents on such terms. The composer of music is in some respects more severely handicapped than any other creative artist. He is never able to give us more than a very clumsy script of his thoughts, a script which is not music until it is translated into sound, and which in many of its details is inherently ambiguous. The interpretation of this script demands intuitive gifts of a specialised order, and however scrupulously these gifts are applied, there is always room for considerable variation of meaning. The composer's picture is thus seen through a mirror which is inaccurate in its detail, and the interpretation of this detail may in accumulation amount to a radical distortion of the intended image. This is just as true of the classics as of contemporary works. It is apparent at once in the idiosyncrasies of a performer who is either out of touch with the traditions handed down from a source originally authoritative, or whose desire to exploit his own individuality makes him a law unto himself. No evangelist can convey to his hearers more than he himself is ready and able to grasp.

Nor do the few cases in which a composer is able to interpret his own work convince us that he is necessarily a good missionary. He is often a victim of the paradox that he can neither interpret himself nor agree with the interpretation of another. His is not the proper detachment essential to the expounding of new ideas, and he is apt to assume that what his intuition finds technically fitting or æsthetically lucid will be clear to his hearers without further argument. The deeper his sincerity the more will misunderstanding take him by surprise. History is full of the bewildered gestures of men whose originality was patent to everyone but themselves. It is the executive artist, as such, who has had to build with care a sense of the new values, who is most likely to present them publicly from an angle related to that of the uninitiate. The part which the

15

performer has to play in the advancement of music cannot be over-emphasised, and his form of specialisation is likely to become more rather than less axiomatic in the art. Nevertheless, this unavoidable process of translation weights the scales heavily against the composer whose style is delicate or distinguished. We shall have to note in due course how the composer may forget that he is dependent upon others for the interpretation of his thoughts. It is so easy to misapprehend the powers or the limitations that properly belong to the human or material forces which he is concerned to use. But it must be admitted with equal honesty that performers can, wilfully or stupidly, make nonsense of what the composer meant to say. More insidiously still, they can select or emphasise just those things which appear to flatter their own taste or their own technique, and thus by the mere exercise of a personal choice they can forestall a public discrimination which might possibly be better than their own. It is perhaps the most difficult of all the functions of criticism to hold the balance between what the composer may be presumed to mean and what the performer elects to say.

A typical example of interpretative technique in which this balance is becoming increasingly difficult to maintain is that associated with modern conducting. The conductor, as we understand the term, is barely a century old. The technique of conducting is hardly more than the product of one or two generations. The conductor was installed in the first place for purposes of discipline, a discipline in early days highly flexible. Singers and players were allowed considerable latitude in the interpretation of their parts, and these parts were as a rule combined in fairly simple fashion. A light hand would hold the concourse together. Then came a progressive complication of aims and means, the effects of which were important in many directions. Composers were inclined to be meticulous in their indications, parts became in themselves less coherent, and it was more and more essential to rely on the conductor to hold the fabric together. Gradually the conductor emerged as a kind of super-performer, whose instrument was itself a complex of individual artists. Exceptional powers of organisation and energy were required, and it is not surprising that some conductors were tempted to think more of themselves than of the music they prepared. The public naturally enjoyed feats of personal ascendancy. It admired the drilled bowing of a score of violins just as it admired the dynamic precision of a military guard. Conductors were extolled for their individual renderings, a conveniently ambiguous term, of the long-suffering classics. Eventually they became the natural arbiters of what should be played as well as of how to play it. They have a power of choice, in the field of works to be studied, which is practically autocratic. Is it unnatural that they should exercise a decided professional taste, and that this taste should be affected by their own technical or administrative point of view ? Conductors often succeed by the handling of masses, by the mastery of complications that can be made effective. He would be a curious colonel who would refuse to augment the strength of his battalion, or shirk the command of other detachments. The contemporary conductor has thus added to his strictly musical function most of those powers which were formerly exercised by the various noble or ignoble directors of the theatre, for example, whose influence on the history of opera was so equivocal. He is far more technically able than they were, but his prerogatives tend to be of the same order. And now that the limelight of the conductor's desk competes with the virtuosities of the solo performer, there is a further temptation to startle the ingenuous rather than to serve a consistent and impersonal ideal. When an artist succeeds by a serene magnetism in giving us the classics without mannerism and without fuss, it is not always certain that a spoiled public will

C

distinguish that which is gold from that which glisters. The orchestral player himself is not often deceived. He knows when a conductor is a pure music-lover. Then he too makes music for its own sake. Under the baton of the less scrupulous he is frequently retained, like so many artists in other spheres, by the confessed necessity of earning his bread.

Such are some of the tangled meshes through which the contemporary reformer has to force his way. The music with which this essay proposes to deal is but a very small fragment, yet it is that fragment which most aggressively challenges the judgement of the amateur, and which will in the long run live or die according to the measure of worth that the unprejudiced can find in it. All progress, and all sane conservation no less, depends on an active minority. It is the single mind which creates. It is the small circle which first comprehends and expounds. Ultimately the fate of a movement will depend on the sincerity of its founders and missionaries as individuals, and on their power to survive as a class. Such pioneers are in a measure compelled to adopt a special attitude, to risk some degree of artistic segregation. The danger is that they may begin to think that peculiarity is a merit in itself. They may then find themselves so high and dry, with reference to the broad stream of experience, that they cease to have any communicable influence. A theory of art is like a theory of life. Its fertility depends at least as much on the breadth of its view as on the acumen of its detail. This alone is a sufficient reason why a discussion of the more daring experiments of our time may well be prefaced by such a sketch of their environment as has been outlined. Only thus can one retain a sense of perspective that may hope to appraise novelties by virtue of standards that are of more than local or momentary importance.

Few by comparison are those who are either actively engaged in the practice of innovation, or whose

18

opportunities give them familiarity with its methods. There are many, however, who are not in the least afraid of reform, could they but grasp its aim and direction. It is to these latter that this book is addressed. It can only offer at best a very rough chart of the ground, necessarily drawn from the angle of a particular and personal experience, though it hopes to indicate some of the problems that appear to lie behind contemporary restlessness. Illustrations will be chosen not so much on account of their ultimate worth, for this would assume a prophetic discernment to which no vestige of a claim is made, as in order to make more clear the general argument. They are finger-posts only, and the amateur who would explore the subject must relate them to the map of his own experience. Without first-hand knowledge of the country, no æsthetic plan of it has any meaning. And there is a further restriction of outlook which always besets the mere discussion of an art. Broadly speaking, the only features in it which can be described consistently are those which are in essence technical. Only on this plane have analytical terms a stable meaning. The rest is in the nature of gossip, which will have as many different associations as there are readers to read it. This literary treatment of activities that are essentially beyond words, this art about art, so to speak, can be of stimulating quality, but it is no substitute for the experience it is concerned to illumine. In no art is this more true than in music; for the fluid nature of its impressions renders them especially difficult to define, while their discussion in isolation may take away the greater part of their meaning. All the arts strive towards an ideal in which form and content are one, in which the thing said and the manner of saying it cannot be separated. Yet any kind of analysis involves at least the partial destruction of this unity. It will be well to acknowledge at once the weaknesses from which our discussion must suffer.

There are many ways of approach to music. For

some its appeal is completely contained in the pure
sensations to which its fabric of sound gives rise. There
is here no question of analysis. The perception of
beauty is unalloyed by intellectual reservations. This
faculty may at one end of the scale degenerate into
raw emotionalism. At the other it is hardly distinguishable from mysticism, from a passive immersion of the
soul in the profound depths of intuitive experience.
The contemplative attitude towards art, notwithstanding its liability to indiscipline or incoherence, is
perhaps the most fundamental of all. It is present to
a degree in every æsthetic impression, though it can
be so variously overlaid with intellectual ideas that it
is apt to be lost sight of. It is a faculty of which
criticism can only with great difficulty take account,
because it is not to be expressed in any terms other than
its own. It suffers, moreover, from a disconcerting
tendency to be eclipsed. It is a commonplace of experience how, with increasing comprehension of artistic
values, the æsthetic sensibility to which they should
minister may become progressively thin. Few of us
would affirm that we can recapture the first thrills
that made a particular experience so memorable. It
sometimes seems as though the more we know about
an art the less we are able to enjoy it. This alone would
account for many of the conflicts of opinion which so
puzzle the inquirer. It is, for example, more than
probable that the appeal of Wagner was in the first
place of this elemental kind. It was those amateurs
who were not obsessed by intellectual predispositions
who accepted Wagner without reserve. It was those
who were presumed to know most about music who
doubted that he was a great musician. Amateur and
professional, to put the distinction crudely, are often
at loggerheads because they are not really discussing
the same facts. To one the whole meaning of music
may depend upon an unreserved sensitiveness which
the other cannot or will not command. Nor is it safe

to assume that an emotion is necessarily inferior because it is acute. This is certainly not true of human experience in general. The honest critic must always be prepared to discover that he cannot see the wood for the trees.

There is happily less risk in attempting to put in its proper place an attitude towards music which is often characteristic of professional and amateur alike. This is the habit of relating it to external experience. To some its appeal lies undoubtedly in its power to suggest impressions which are associated with other activities of life or thought. To these all music is to some extent programme-music. It is not that the music must necessarily embody a concrete story, though this is frequently the case, but that the hearer cannot remain a passive agent in the reciprocal process of comprehension. He actively grasps or invents a meaning that must be so far actual as to invoke at least a sense of representation, of drama, historical it may be, or graphic, or literary. It may be realistic or it may be vague. It may be clear as a picture, or it may be no more than a dim surmise. There are those for whom the Moonlight Sonata, for instance, is definitely enriched by the suggestions that its posthumous title conveys. This attitude is unfortunately beset by a constant temptation to ask for more and more realism in relation to the external imagery. There will be much to say of this demand later, but it must be admitted that it is both a legitimate and a potent factor in the appreciation of music, and often of the very best music. That music can be related to many other forms of experience, to poetry, to landscape, to drama, and so forth, is one of its glories, and it would be a deadening philosophy that should proscribe a faculty because it is capable of abuse. What must be insisted on is that the artist himself shall know what is proper to his art and what is not. Moonshine in music is the prerogative of the listener, not of the creator.

There remains, finally, the factor of technique. Technique is primarily the concern of the student, of a particular kind of spectator. It deals with internal values in art, considered frankly as lines, colours, masses, or sounds, as the case may be. Many of its elements are capable of definition. They have their foundations in tradition, their justification in accumulated experience. The technical view is admittedly a narrow one, but like every other attitude it is never completely isolated. No man's reaction to art can be purely mystical, or purely external, or purely technical. Whether he knows it or not, he will partake in some measure of them all. Thus technique will find itself confronted with problems that cannot be divorced from less material factors. Somehow the inspiration of the artist has to get itself materially expressed, whatever may be its initial purity of spirit. Material expression will have its own qualities, its own defects, and the mastery of these problems is a technical gift. Yet the technical analyst must never forget that a creative faculty may transcend its technique, and inspiration may find expression in spite of almost any degree of clumsiness. The broken utterance may, indeed, be itself an earnest of conviction. It is too great a facility which is more often fatal.

MELODY AND RHYTHM*
O for the good old tunes of Strauss and Debussy !
Punch.

THE search for logical principles, or for the less
consistent intuitions that more frequently
underlie the practice of an art, may be carried
to the point of pedantry. Yet without some measure
of analysis of this kind there can hardly be clear thinking. Take, for example, the very rough truth that
music, in its elements, consists of certain conventional
variations of pitch arranged in some kind of measured
time Quantities and qualities of sound are here omitted,
and the definition is thus for our ears a mere skeleton.
Without variations of quantity and quality in the
sounds produced, music is for us comparatively lifeless.
What is now commonly understood as expression
would hardly exist under such limitations. Yet there
has been a music which throve on a very crude apparatus of this nature. The early organs, for instance, paid

---

* As this is not a text-book, nor intended primarily for the specialist,
I have normally used the word *rhythm* in the sense now commonly
attached to it. It means that framework of regulated and recurrent
accents which is the time basis of classical and modern music alike.
A near analogy would be the accentual metre of English verse spoken
with the rigidity of a metronome. The non-accentual rhythm of early
polyphony, and the various meanings attached to the word in arts
other than music, are now more akin to what in music is called phrasing.
I sympathise with the specialist who may find this ambiguity dis-
tracting, but I hope the context will make my own view clear. It is
just this change of attitude towards time-values which is the main
subject of the present chapter. If ever we get back to the earlier conception of rhythm we shall probably have to invent a new word for it.
In this discussion I have thus ventured to contrast rhythm with rhapsody, in the hope that rhapsody will suggest to the contemporary
reader that freedom which the word rhythm has lost.

little attention to detailed variations of quantity or quality of sound, and classical organ music is still best interpreted in comparatively broad masses of flat tone. The characteristic repose and grandeur of it are ruined if the attention is too much usurped by artifices of expression of the modern sort. Even in that music which is able to command the remarkably expressive powers of the voice, there have been schools of thought in which these possibilities were strictly disciplined. The art of the chancel, from which so many of the major traditions of music are historically derived, preserved and in a measure still preserves a technical heritage in which violent contrasts of quantity or quality of sound are æsthetically out of place. The contemplative mood which prevails in the purest forms of religious music cannot properly encourage the distractions of too dynamic a style. The beauty of music can be enshrined in factors far more simple than we of this complicated age are apt to assume.

The broad division of music into elements of pitch and elements of time is therefore strictly real so far as it goes, and the concentration of interest on one or other of these factors does actually provide a certain scale of values. Variations of pitch become, in their simplest form, melody, and melody is therefore one of the fundamental values in music. Is this also true of time ? Can there be a music which is timeless ?

Crudely considered, no. It is the peculiar quality of music, as opposed to the arts of painting, sculpture and architecture, that time is one of its fundamental dimensions. In time is its life, and for every problem of musical thought the question of when is inextricably bound up with the question of how. But if this time is understood to mean some clock-like form of measurement, some provision of regular and recurrent intervals in the time sense, then music is far from giving an unqualified answer. To the ear time can only be calculated by regular pulsations, whether real or

24

imaginary. The time of music, however, was originally more strictly akin to the time of speech. It often asked for no more than what in prose is known as quantity. Measurement in the metrical sense was not essential to it. Its time may indeed be compared with the space of the graphic arts. It is always possible to make measurements of a drawing. One can subject it intellectually to a form of squared paper. But to demand that points of interest or of conjunction shall occur at so many precise and measurable intervals of distance is a negation of all that is normally meant by graphic art. Even in those graphic decorations which are nearest to pure geometry, as in the carved panel or the woven carpet, it is just the details and associations of spatial mass which are not geometrical, which give a design its artistic life. In similar fashion speech may be measured, and by a suitable arrangement of words may be made into verse. But versification is not poetry. Nor is the measurement of time music. It is precisely when singer and listener are alike unconscious of the pulse of time that purest song is achieved.

These distinctions require occasionally to be emphasised anew. Measured time is the parent of the dynamic rhythm of to-day. Is this rhythm an essential factor in the art of music in the same sense or to the same extent that melody is ? Even with regard to the science of pitch, music has sometimes striven to avoid too exact or too final a definition of scales and intervals, though here it is a matter of physical fact that there exist certain consonances which will always provide standards, should standards be needed. There are no analogous standards of time. Time is the flux in which music is immersed. It can be measured, but all such measurements are arbitrary.

As a rough approximation it may be said that until the end of the sixteenth century rhythm as we now interpret it did not exist in serious music. For by far the greater part of recorded history music in its highest

25

forms was almost exclusively vocal. There was not, as indeed there still is not, any instrument which within the range proper to the voice can equal it either in beauty of sound or in subtlety and depth of expression. And the voice is not naturally rhythmic. Measured music of a kind it can and did produce, but its natural time is fluid and intuitive, like the time of thought, of emotion, of sensation. It is not the time of regular and mechanical pulses. The play of thought is free, and speech is no more than a precipitation of thought. The accents and quantities of a language are in origin the expression of mental and emotional stresses to which the common experience of men has given a common value. They are articulate but none the less fluid representations of experience. In moments of high sensitiveness they may be imagined, as it were, in combination with the solemnity or with the passion of metrical rhythm. But this rhythm is not inherent. It is the art of the poet which chooses thus to crystallise a peculiarly vivid impression. In like fashion may music organise in the time sense the elements of its melodic diction. It may subject them to the conscious purposes of an artistic proportion. Speech and song are closely related. They have in origin the same physical organs. They have or had similar intuitive aims. That they should also have a common flexibility was the most natural thing in the world, and it probably never even occurred to the serious composers of the middle ages that their art might one day bind itself in what to them would have appeared to be the gross chains of persistent rhythm.

What is sometimes called the tyranny of the bar-line, which is another name for the ubiquity of stereotyped accents and rhythms, is a comparatively mushroom growth of the last three hundred years. When the chests of viols and other essentially melodic instruments first reached, some three hundred years ago, a stage of development which could no longer be ignored by serious composers, there were two marked types of music in existence, neither of which was pure, from the instrumental point of view. On the one hand there was the whole body of cultivated music, which in its essential features was vocal. Its purest forms had been developed by the mediaeval church, and so far as alien influences had affected its technique they had involved little more than a very flexible alliance with Latin prose. It was essentially a contemplative art, and it was in practice confined for the most part to those who had a special skill in it or a special vocation towards it. Though it had notorious abuses, these had not challenged the melodic purity of its style. Even when it used verse, either sacred or secular, as a pivot for its architectural forms, it treated the devices of poetic metre with the greatest licence. Much of it was what we should now call *coloratura*, melody, that is, of the most decorative or rhapsodic type. Though its idioms became in time more highly organised, and though the combination of voices noticeably confined the freedom of individual parts, there was no rigid framework of rhythm, and single voices expressed their values according to the demands of their own melodic line. It was to this music that the viols, with their power of sustained and vocal melody, appeared to be well adapted, and to this music they were in the first place frequently devoted.

Alternatively there was the music which in all societies had served as a handmaid to dancing. Music thus permeated with strong and regular rhythms had played a vigorous though somewhat ambiguous part in the artistic life of the people. It had naturally been associated with every variety of primitive instrument. When, therefore, the hour was ripe for a music that should be purely instrumental, dance-music was a powerful aspirant. In the music belonging to this crucial period which we still possess, it is easy to trace the sharp struggle which took place between the voice and the

27

dance for the command of the new instruments. Gradually but inexorably we can see the persistent rhythms of the dance subduing step by step the more melodic and polyphonic freedom of the older style. In the end the dance gained an overwhelming victory.

It has been noticed in our own day how difficult it is to imagine keyboard music in terms other than those of the hand. It is almost impossible to think spontaneously, for example, in terms suited to the pianola. Every chord and every ornament occurs first to the imagination as hand-music. New forms are not created by a sudden exercise of will. The fancy responds freely only to that with which its associations are already intimate. Of this the birth of classical instrumental music is a striking case. One can see the Elizabethans, in the Fitzwilliam collection for example, vainly trying to create a new instrumental art. Their curious and whimsical experiments and variations are so many attempts not to confine the new apparatus within the old forms. They failed. Their successes were either instrumental madrigals or confessed adaptations of dance tunes. No other forms existed. No new form could be suddenly created. For a time the Prelude and Fugue, the one a rhapsodic extemporisation, the other a form with vocal antecedents, gathered and retained a certain prestige. Ornamental recitative never completely died out. Dramatic or contemplative prose simply could not be danced, and the associations or inflections of vocal narration could sometimes be used with marked effect in purely instrumental works. The reader will recall in this connexion examples so late in date as the D minor Sonata and the Ninth Symphony of Beethoven. But these were drops in the ocean. From the standpoint of mediaeval polyphony Bach, Handel, Haydn, Mozart, and Beethoven were all alike writers of dance music. The old suites of dances took the more non-committal titles of Sonata and Symphony, but there was no break in rhythmic or formal continuity. The voice itself, once the supreme arbiter about what was proper to the art, was gradually subjected to the same all-pervading influence, and the pronounced effect of regular and recurring accents became a marked factor in music of every kind. The momentous nature of this change cannot be exaggerated. It was probably as complete a revolution as has ever occurred in the history of any art. Omit the voice from the music of the preceding centuries, and hardly anything is left. Omit it from the music which has since commanded our allegiance, and a whole library of masterpieces would remain. Yet the roots of the art are still vocal, are still melodic, and a theory of music which forgets or ignores this truth can have no sure foundations*.

Nor was the rhythm of the dance alone incorporated. The very patterns of the dance invaded music of all kinds. To us there seems to be something inherently natural in the normal design of a classical tune. The melodies of Haydn and Mozart in particular, of the early Beethoven, and of the host of men who have imitated these classics, appear to fall intuitively into certain four-square schemes of phrases. There is a first half which proceeds almost by formula to the dominant, and a second half which just as inevitably returns to the tonic. Patterns of this kind, whether melodic or harmonic, are almost axiomatic in the technique of the

* In thus ascribing our modern conception of rhythm to the influence of dance music, I am recording what appears to have been the most direct agent. But it was not the only one. There had long been a metric *harmony*, in which moments of harmonic interest (discords and changes of harmony) had alternated with moments of harmonic relaxation (resolutions and movements within the same chord). But this interest lay at first solely in the harmony itself. No accent was involved. Melody therefore could and did ignore this framework completely, so far as its own internal values were concerned, and this was just as true of many melodies as of one. There is no doubt, however, that the concentration of harmonic thought on a metrical basis, a tradition which of course still persists, helped greatly to justify and encourage the adoption of a framework of regular accents.

period. Yet it is highly doubtful whether they have any foundation in pure music as such. Historically they are certainly dance patterns. The diagrams of country-dance figures which the old dancing masters used to publish would serve with extraordinary fidelity as graphs of classical tunes. The dancer by a chain of related figures reaches as it were the opposite pole of his orbit, his steps being synchronised with the rhythm and phrasing of the tune, which at this point reaches its half-way close. Dancer and tune alike return to the starting-point by a parallel series of steps. This is the full close. It is hardly conceivable that melodic form of so pronounced a type should have been accidentally evolved from an earlier style that showed little or no trace of it. There is an alternative explanation, and that is the possible influence of metrical verse. This, however, could in the first place affect only vocal music, and we have seen that the voice was becoming the slave rather than the master of these fashions. The troubadour would no doubt be inclined to compose for his metrical ballad a metrical tune, but if our folk-songs are trustworthy evidence, there was considerable independence even here. One of the greatest charms of many of these songs is the way in which they handle so delightfully the natural flexibilities of melodic outline. The form of a metrical ballad is not essential to pure melody, and there is no evidence that the Elizabethans, for instance, consciously sought their chief models in this direction. Vocally they worshipped at the shrine of the contrapuntists, whose art had little to do with pattern of this kind. Indeed, the pressure towards symmetrical melodic form has in later times come from the composer rather than from the poet. Music is full of songs built on ironbound patterns, and it is often impossible to find in such melodies anything approaching the freedom, either of metre or sense, which belongs to an intelligent interpretation of the words.

30

Yet beyond dance patterns, and beyond verse metres, there is another influence which has consistently weighted the scales in favour of these rhythmic and symmetrical values, as against the more flexible intuitions of pure melody. Rhythmic tyranny in music is very largely the fruit of executive discipline. The bar-line was a device of discipline. It had no logical place in a solo performance, but it materially assisted the executive combination of voices or instruments by giving individuals an indication as to the propriety or otherwise of their respective ideas of pace. It naturally tended to mark phrases, but it had at first little accentual and no rhythmic significance. A near parallel to these primitive bar-lines are the letters or numbers that are now placed at frequent intervals to facilitate the rehearsal of concerted works. They have nothing to do with the music, but they often occur at well-defined points in the structure, and they serve as the bar-line did to guide or recall the erring performer. When the bar-line began to be regularly spaced, it was inevitable that it should gather an accentual value, and its combination with dance rhythms made it the natural indicator of a strong following beat. To this beat we are all disciplined, and it is notorious how difficult we find the performance of Elizabethan or earlier works in which the bar-line has no accentual meaning. To us it seems unnatural that a word or a note should be given the prominence due to its quantity or sense, irrespective of its position in the bar. Thus discipline has supported rhythms of automatic regularity, and the modern problem of handling large numbers of performers has magnified the practice unceasingly. A few have always protested, and there has lately been a decided reversion towards flexibility, for example, in massed singing of the Psalms. But chanting was an art of the choir, not of the nave. Flexible chanting requires a degree of practice and intimacy which is beyond large congregations. This particular problem has given birth to that curious musical phenomenon, the Anglican chant. Analogous difficulties arise in every one of our musical formations, skilled or otherwise.

For the skill of the individual does not emancipate him. Conductors of the most accomplished orchestras and choirs are driven by the mere problems of size to exact an ever stricter discipline. The constitution of the modern orchestra shows in epitome the evolution of this rhythmic ascendancy. A group of solo wind instruments is combined with a chorus of strings. The wind players therefore enjoy a certain freedom of interpretation. The strings are perforce drilled. And yet we know that every one of these string players is in his private capacity an individual and an artist. Bach used to mobilise the less proficient players that were at hand, and employ them as a chorus to his nucleus of skilled men. One is tempted to wonder if he foresaw an organisation in which fifty or sixty players of the highest attainments might be virtually compelled to hide every trace of their individual powers of interpretation Would he deny that under such conditions an artist's latent sensitiveness might desert him, or that such a system might select and maintain the efficient rather than the inspired ? The infantry of the vocal chorus is in like case. One tenor in fifty has exactly one chance in fifty of contributing some element of distinction to the performance of a masterpiece. There is no escape from the dilemma. We demand effects of mass. Mass formations are the product of drill. The apotheosis of drill is rhythm.

It is not suggested that the massive orchestras and still more massive choirs of our day have no high place in music. They are capable of a grandeur and breadth of appeal that can be obtained in no other way. Nor is so powerful an expressive agent as the explosive pulsation of rhythm to be dismissed as inherently damaging to the art. The problem is one of comparative values. These effects are bought at a price. If that price entails an executive discipline which undermines the more æsthetic gifts of the performer, or if it tends to encourage the cruder and more primitive reactions of the listener, then what is gained in immediate power may be more than lost in decline of quality. And when standards of appreciation are shifted on to a rhythmic or quantitative base, there is at least a risk that the purity of music in the melodic sense will progressively degenerate. That we are already in the toils of such a movement is shown by the part which the exploitation of rhythm as such now plays in the appraisement of music. Education itself has embraced it. There are not a few systems of musical training, of high repute, which appear to affirm that the modern view of rhythm is a kind of royal road in the art. To Bach such an idea would have seemed too childish for discussion. To Palestrina it would have been literally meaningless. Are we quite so sure of our ground ? Can their music, or that of our own Elizabethans, be properly approached by any conceivable theory of persistent rhythms ? This modern sense of rhythm is perhaps more generally diffused than the gift of song, but to suggest that the mechanical beating of time is a fundamental accomplishment in the art of music is completely to misapprehend what has hitherto been accounted its peculiar glory. And if melody is to be subjected to alien theories of this kind, then the supreme influence of technical purity in the practice and fertility of an art will be forgotten or ignored. Dancing is one art, music is another. The two can be combined. So can music and poetry. But let us at least be clear which is which.

The intuitions of Bach in this respect, as indeed in so many others, are for us exemplary. He lived at a time when the rhythmic notation of music was already universal. He accepted the conventions of regular and recurrent stress accents. What view of the function of these conventions does his work support ?

D

In the first place there is a considerable portion of his work in which the factor of rhythm, in its more dynamic forms, plays hardly any part. Not only the recitatives, but many complete and characteristic movements, of which the G minor Organ Fantasia (see Ex. 37) will serve as a type, have an atmosphere that no stretching of terms can describe as rhythmic in the accentual sense. In them the stately passage of time may be measured, but there is no crude appeal to the pulse of it as such. Bach often exploits a rhythmic pattern, but it is always assimilated melodically. It is expressed in melodic terms. Even in those passages where the rhythm is peculiarly striking, there is generally a simultaneous melodic line of such distinction that the two can hardly be thought of apart. And as Bach's technique was essentially a weaving of melodies, the rhythmic patterns are soon overlaid and complicated by the detail of other voices. The chosen formula is dissolved in a higher synthesis of texture or architecture. Rhythm is not an end in itself. This is the gulf between his day and ours. Holst begins his Fugal Overture Op. 40, thus :

Bach did *not* announce the C minor Fugue thus :

This particular work is perhaps not one by which Holst sets great store. It is quoted because it is symptomatic of our day. It is fugal only intermittently, but fugal or no, it is predominantly rhythmic, sometimes exclusively so. It is presumably a *jeu d'esprit*. His Fugal

34

Concerto is conceived on lines more essentially melodic, though in this work too there is a frequent shifting of interest on to the more frankly rhythmic side.

It may be well, however, to avoid for the moment the extremes of either direction, and to ask what was the average reaction of Bach to these factors. The following is taken from the beginning of the *St. Matthew Passion*. In studying this and other examples of the period, it is important to discount the more dynamic *interpretation* of music characteristic of our modern handling of masses. Let the style speak for itself :

Bach is sometimes more rhythmic than this, sometimes less. Here the rhythmic bass is a background against which the melodic texture is developed. It was on the rhapsodic flow of melodies that Bach's attention was intuitively concentrated, and in this matter, as in so many others, he achieved a balance in the treatment of basic ideas which is, for his epoch, final and complete. He embraced accentual rhythms, but never at the expense of melody, just as he explored harmonies, but never at the expense of part-writing. There could be no fitter starting-point for the analysis of contemporary tendencies than a consciousness of the values which Bach accepted and which have so well stood the test of time.

Against the rigid versification of melody Bach's whole art was a protest. Even in the dance suites it is remarkable how the four-squareness of the dance is never allowed to become conventional. His Allemands are Preludes, his Gigues are Fugues, his Corantos are of every formal type, while out of the Sarabande he

35

produced movements of quiet and rhapsodic beauty that are only to be compared with the slow movements of Beethoven. Melody was the raw material of Bach's genius, and melody not of the metric type, but fluid, rhapsodic, free. No considerations of pattern, as such, confined the spontaneity of his inspiration. And to this view might Handel too in substantial measure subscribe. He had less than Bach's integrity, but he had a great and glowing warmth, and his style was at its best so monumental that there was not often room in it either for crude rhythms or for pretty tunes.

At this point the reader will invoke Scarlatti, Haydn, and Mozart, the melodic Beethoven, and Schubert, and Brahms. Were these not melodists, versified or no ? It must be admitted that in one important respect they represent a secession from the values of Bach. Up to and including Bach it may be said that the evolution of serious music obeyed two related laws ; namely, that music is melody, and that two melodies are better than one. From this logic his successors receded. They gradually learnt to distil their melodic gifts into a single line. Concentrating on this, they lost Bach's sense of the equally vital significance of every other strand of thought. Hence arose all sorts of ambiguities, rhythmic, harmonic and formal, which were comparatively alien to Bach. Yet melodists they remained, and we still think of them as finding their highest forms of expression in what had always been accounted the essential stuff of music. But of their versification there can be no question. Are they for this reason to be set on a lower plane than Bach, than Palestrina ? This question suggests the familiar discussion about the respective merits of epic and lyric poetry. A working hypothesis is not hard to find. Whether melody as such is versified or no, is comparatively immaterial. The important fact is that versification is not poetry. Many of the critical failures of the nineteenth century were due to the way in which

36

the prestige of Haydn and Mozart had deceived men into thinking that the versifying of a melody was as important as the æsthetic quality of it. The melody of Bach was in this matter like the melody of Shakespeare's blank verse. The melody of Mozart is the Shakespearean lyric. There can be no dispute concerning the supreme value of both. Danger lies in the circumstance that a superficial mind can sometimes disguise its poverty by clever versifying. It is more difficult to hide the poverty of bad blank verse.

Symmetrical patterns may, of course, be a feature of the harmony or of the ornamentation, rather than of the melodic line itself. In any event their value is a derived value, not an intrinsic one. It was the progressive misconception of these distinctions which led to the day when men said that the formal lilt of Verdi was music,

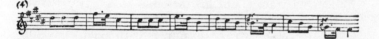

while the rhapsody of Wagner was not:

Between Mozart and Beethoven there was a divergence of aim in many respects, but the melodic technique of the latter grew out of that of the former. If we may venture to take one of Beethoven's ideas and frame it as Mozart might have done, the product would be essentially symmetrical, like the tune of a dance or the verse of a ballad.

37

Beethoven actually wrote the following (*Symphony No. 5*):

(7)

Apart from the harmonic interest which he accumulated under this pattern, is it not clear that the more epic Beethoven, so to speak, was thus bursting the melodic bonds in which Haydn and Mozart had found it possible to express themselves? This versified development of Beethoven could be made to lead either to a new theme or to a kind of peak in the melodic contour. Frequently phrases of this nature became by condensation more and more dynamic until what had been a vocal melody changed into a rhythmic figure. Beethoven was enlarging the sweep, as it were, of the Mozartian stanza, and his melodies frequently assisted in this way the building of a symphonic architecture. Compare these two last examples with Bach's melodic lines in Ex. 3, and the history of a century is clear. Wagner inherited Beethoven's device and used it extensively in his running comments on a moving dramatic situation. In the hands of the lesser symphonists of the nineteenth century it became almost a mechanical formula.

Rhythmically, Haydn and Mozart accepted without question the fashions of their day, but there was a certain delicacy, both in the ideals for which they worked and in the somewhat cloistered civilisation of which they were ornaments, which encouraged dynamic restraint. The lilt of their rhythms is often undisguised, but it is rarely aggressive. No such reservation can be made with respect to Beethoven. He was not only rhythmic, but violently rhythmic. He did deliberately appeal to the pulse as such, and he had no hesitation in developing to the utmost every dynamic factor of

38

which his instruments were capable. Yet there are two observations respecting Beethoven's methods which are pertinent to our present point of view. In the first place, his most untiring rhythms have a habit of falling into what one may perhaps call a melodic procession. There often rises over and above them, as it were, an arc of melody:

(8)

And in the second place, even where persistent rhythms seem to pile up a crescendo of purely dynamic excitement, they do, in Beethoven, find a musician equal to the task of creating that purer music which alone could justify such tremendous preparations. In the Overtures to *Coriolanus* and *Leonora No. 3*, in the Fifth, Seventh, and Ninth Symphonies, to name a few of Beethoven's more dynamic *tours de force*, it is the serene and unqualified beauty of his melodies which relieves and purges the intensity of his rhythms. Rob Beethoven of his melodies and the rest is chaos. His imagination was equal to his fervour. His method is poison to minds of average talent. And the same is true of the dynamic Wagner. The 'Ride of the Valkyries' is musical champagne. It is his sustained melodic beauty which is the measure of Wagner's power. If the imitator cannot match the *Siegfried Idyll*, rhythmic virtuosity is a poor substitute. As to this latter work, and the same is true of *Die Meistersinger* as a whole, it may be said that there is not, since Bach, anything that can compete with it, with reference to those ideals of melodic outline and texture which, had we chosen to follow them, might have given us the modern equivalent of Bach's technique. And these were the

39

ideals which Wagner, like Bach, could sustain through the long periods of a major work. To sum up : the safe way is the way of Bach ; rhythm, whether considered as a convention of accents or as a system of patterns, being idealised in melody. The dangerous way is the way of Beethoven, for the justificat on of a rhythmic or formal pyramid will depend on the supreme quality of the melodic relief. It were better in this case to make quite sure beforehand that the requisite degree of melodic power is at hand.

These fundamental reactions have been dealt with at some length, because the attitude of contemporary tendencies towards them can only be described as chaotic. Before it is possible to have any consistent views on what music is doing, it is well to know what music is. Our age is an experimental one, artistically as well as materially. We have few settled convictions, except perhaps the negative one that all the old formulae are doomed. In this matter of rhythm versus melody we are still in a measure under the spell of Beethoven, though it might be fairer to say that we have adopted just so much of him as a narrower talent could imitate. There were some, even among his contemporaries, who viewed Beethoven's violence with misgiving. To them it seemed that the more æsthetic significance of music might be engulfed in waves of physical or nervous excitement. Nor was this fear unjustified. Never before had vehemence been able to attach itself to a classical standard. The percussion of the modern orchestra is a material embodiment of this post-Beethoven orthodoxy. It was only to be expected that these vigorous means would be used for purposes of dynamic illustration. The dramatic conceptions of opera and stage-music proceeded to feed this desire, and the programme music of the symphonic poem added fuel to the flames. Finally, in our day, the ballet has exerted direct influence in the same direction, and it almost seems as if the subjection of music to external

40

ideas, of which perhaps dancing is the ringleader, has become the incurable malady of the art.

Yet it is difficult to believe that there are not many who feel the discomfort of this drift. When Strauss began the Battle in *Ein Heldenleben* thus,

proceeding to pound his drums unmercifully for long passages at a stretch, there were some, and among them many of his admirers, who began to ask, to what end? And when Holst begins *The Planets* ('Mars') by a twentieth-century variant of the same notion, and

pursues it indefatigably, and when any other composer piles up a rhythmic apparatus until its vehemence almost stuns the judgement, may not one very properly ask, to what end? That this is war is not even a half-truth. We smile at Purcell's little realisms of this kind. So will posterity smile at us. In any event what has music to do with such simplicities? War is a state of the soul, and only in some form of psychic translation can it come into music at all. It is not to be represented by vicarious marching. It is drill which is rhythmic, not fighting. The vicarious march, and its near relative, the vicarious dance, find a ready response in the public pulse, and they can be exploited to the verge of hysteria. None the less, however, are they the temporary tricks of the trade. The intuition of the cultivated music-lover has indeed always told him that rhythmic violence must in the end defeat itself. The twentieth century can make more actual noise than the nineteenth.

41

and it can therefore offer what for a moment seems to be a more imposing climax. But it is only the big drum's superiority over the little one, and the more noise it makes the more tiresome it is.

Admitting, however, that it may be impossible to dismiss this infectious tendency towards dynamic forms of statement, there are yet certain obvious ways of avoiding too crude a display of them. Mechanical rhythms can be ignored, as Palestrina and the Elizabethans ignored them, and as indeed so many of the deepest and most intimate things in the music of every age have substantially ignored them. The march of time may be accepted, but no direct appeal made to the pulse of it as such. In this connexion it is perhaps worth noting how partial were some of the composers of the past to bars of great length. Frameworks of eight, nine, or twelve slow beats are frequently to be found. This may seem at first sight to be no more than a technical fashion. But there may be more in it than that. Long, slow, and complicated bars of this kind reduce the lilt of rhythm to a minimum. There can be little consciousness of it under such conditions. Beethoven indeed occasionally gives up altogether the task of barring a rhapsodic passage. What he was then trying to say could not be reduced to such rigid terms. It was this same bid for freedom which evolved the cadenza in its various forms, and above all in its form of rhapsodic *coloratura*. It is easy to scoff at the abuse which shallow composers and shallow artists made of this convention. Ideally it stands for a fundamental æsthetic truth. The beauties of pure tune, combined with the beauties of pure tone, represent something as near to pure music as we are ever likely to get. The instrumental cadenza was intended to offer a similar feast. It was to be music unfettered either by the angularities of form or by the discipline of ensemble.

A second method is to avoid the rawness of regular accents by introducing syncopations and subtleties of

42

every kind. This, of course, was what Bach did,

and Purcell,

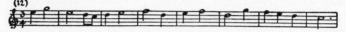

and a hundred other composers. The conventional framework is felt, or there could be no breaking of it. There is no syncopation of this kind in Palestrina. But the conventional pulsations are in these two examples only a background against which the fancy plays unreservedly. Schumann sometimes carried this method to a point at which the cross accents destroy the framework altogether. His experiments are occasionally in the nature of eye-music. So is the end of Beethoven's Op. 106, so far as the barring is concerned. These are but extreme symptoms of a general disposition. And it is interesting to observe how this method of avoiding rhythmic monotony has spread even to the most popular forms of dance or song. The Waltz always used cross accents of Schumannesque type, but in our own day the inherent monotony of two- and four-beat rhythms has justified, to hearers of negligible discrimination, syncopations of considerable violence. The most pachydermatous ear will in the end revolt against the pneumatic hammer. The unfortunate mental patient who beats his head ' because it is so nice to leave off ' is not a rare phenomenon. The more sensitive reach this stage a little sooner ; that is all. The beginning of *Till Eulenspiegel* shows Strauss' subtlety in this matter, and very delightful it is.

So is Elgar's clever analysis of eight quavers in *The Dream of Gerontius.*

(14)

The golden rule is that rhythmic devices of this kind should never be allowed to lose their freshness either by too crude a statement or too many repetitions. Delicacy and variety are the spice of them. They are, when combined with pace and subtlety, the comedy of music.

Thirdly, there is the invention of new basic rhythms. The slow movement of Tschaikowsky's *Pathetic* symphony set everybody trying to think and beat in fives. Tschaikowsky's time is really two plus three, just as *Mars* (Ex. 10) is three plus two. The slow movement of Chopin's C minor Sonata is much nearer to a true five-group. Holst, however, in *The Perfect Fool*, has succeeded admirably, and the happy spontaneity of this example is clearly due to the fact that it is conceived melodically. The phrases fall easily into the framework. They are the framework, in reality. That Holst sometimes notates it as if it were three plus two makes no difference to its smooth effect on the ear.

(15)

We may here be within sight of a formula that may in time be treated with the intuitive freedom of the old two- and three-groups. Seven-beat experiments are not yet so fortunate.

44

The following is also from *The Perfect Fool.*

Here Holst is perhaps educating both himself and
us into the belief that we can be made to think alternate
threes and fours without constraint. That is why
there is as much rhythm as melody in the phrases, and
they are repeated for the same reason. Pure sevens
do not enter into the matter. But even if they did it
would not affect the principles we are concerned to
illustrate. Children can be taught to beat elevens and
thirteens, or two or three prime numbers at once. As
mental gymnastics such exercises have their value. But
all regular and recurring accents are as such dangerously
monotonous, their effect depending on physical reactions of doubtful or diminishing worth. There is
then a strong temptation to reinforce them more and
more violently. Yet it is only when a rhythm has
become practically intuitive that there can be much
real musical fertility in it, for only then can the mind
be left free to enjoy vastly more productive ideas.
We see Stravinsky and other contemporary writers
of ballet-music driven to devise ever more complicated
rhythmic formulae in order to avoid the commonplace.
The full circle of their progress may even lead back to
timelessness in the mediæval sense. It sometimes seems
a pity that we cannot take a short cut and have done
with the problem. There are contemporary composers
who do quote from and imitate mediæval melodies of
this kind. Even Stravinsky, in spite of his devotion to
ballet and his extraordinary rhythmic intuitions, appears
really to be searching for some such relief in passages
like the following from *Pétrouchka.*

(17)

This is the tyranny of the barline with a vengeance
Two simultaneous obsessions seem to be involved;
an inability to think of a barline without a following
accent, and a conviction that only barlines can make
accents intelligible. There is a large mixture of optical
illusion too. The ear cares nothing for complicated
barring. Its flair is for phrasing and accent. It is an
odd bid for flexibility which binds the offending restriction tighter and tighter. Surely the actual music
of the above example could be expressed a little less
algebraically. Suppose Brahms had been afraid that his
phrasing might be overlooked unless he presented the
melody, say, of the first movement of the third symphony in some such guise as the following :

(18)

Brahms had more faith and more restraint. But then
he had not danced himself giddy.

Conventions are proverbially irksome to the æsthetic
temperament, and the melodic gift has often rebelled
against the metrical view of song. Thus Wagner found
it increasingly difficult to express himself within the
four-square patterns that had become almost synony-
mous with melody in the minds of his contemporaries.
Thus our own pioneers, when their reactions seek for

intimacy of thought, cannot or will not write what are now commonly called tunes. Our ideals are, at their best, rhapsodic, and Wagner, Debussy, and Stravinsky embody them.

It is sometimes objected that such melodies do not ' go anywhere'. But then the melodies of the middle ages, not to mention the sustained flights of Bach, did not go anywhere in this colloquial sense. The formal element in melody is, as we have tried to show, no standard of its worth. The identification of inspiration with pattern is a confusion of principles. What may, however, safely be said is that the power to write convincing rhapsody is a rare gift. Let there be the smallest failure of inspiration, and the composer is meandering. It is a most exacting form of art in which genius must never be intermittent. There have been many minor poets whose work has survived by virtue of the charm which lies in a neat thought neatly expressed. The epics of the second-rate are of all poems the least alive. Similarly, what was known as the Italian form of opera, consisting of a chain of lyrical ideas each neatly rounded off, has served to keep alive and grateful the memory of many a composer who had no claim to the first rank. It is Wagnerian opera without Wagner which is the deadliest of all failures. Our contemporaries who rhapsodise must therefore be given the credit of accepting formidable risks. The problem of the metrical tune

47

is not so severe. One slight idea of real distinction, combined with an instinct for proportion or decoration, may be enough. Such is the genesis of some of the most exquisite melodies of Mozart, or of those composers whose gifts approached the quality of his.

(22)

These gems are comparable to the magic idea enshrined in a perfect lyric. It would be absurd to suggest that in any absolute fashion they are to be set lower than the inspired march of a great epic. But their scale is different, they are less extended, and however impossible it may be to choose between beauties of different kinds, the consensus of opinion has always leaned towards a verdict that makes the power of sustained intensity an attribute of the greatest minds. We need not belittle the melodies of Mozart in exalting those of Bach, but there is a factor of size, of depth, of range, call it what one will, which may express itself less convincingly in a dress of formal neatness than in the more elemental fervour of rhapsody.

But let neither pattern nor absence of pattern be accepted as criteria: there remains the melodic quality itself. The vocal origin of melody has associated it with impressions of smoothness, with what is technically known as conjoint motion, and there is a point at which angularity destroys it. Speed too has important reactions. The reader who is interested in the analysis of these factors may like to observe the transformation that occurs when we take Verdi's Ex. 4 and give it the slower speed, the less jerky rhythm, and the more careful dress of Mozart's Ex. 22. It is remarkable how near we can thus approach to the serenity and repose of Mozart himself (Ex. 23).

48

In like manner, compare the following examples. The first two are from *Till Eulenspiegel*, the third from *Tristan*.

The first is whimsical, the second is charming, the third is—well, whatever it was that made the touch of Wagner bring new worlds before us. The ultimate stature of an artist seems indeed to resolve itself into terms that are as simple as they are intangible. It is an intuition, an attitude, a word, a gesture, a line, a few quiet notes, and the magic is consummate.

The use of the larger intervals is possible, but they must either be familiar in themselves, or the ear must be given leisure to adjust itself smoothly. Compare a line from Wagner's *Faust* Overture with one from Strauss's *Salome*. Further comparisons are available in the examples quoted in the chapters on Texture.

E

It is no use attempting to disguise the fact that melody is quite literally song. The more difficult it is to sing a phrase, either actually or imaginatively, the less it partakes of the essential nature of melody, or as some would say, of music. Our ears and our æsthetic reactions are in this matter not instrumentally but vocally attuned. Two or three generations are a trifle in the evolution of faculties so inbred as these. The normal ear recognises as music only that which it can to some degree assimilate, and as the first primitive endowment of this faculty was vocal, so have the accumulated impressions it has since gathered been consistently related to that origin. We are all singers, whether we know it or not, and singers we shall for some long time yet remain.

Now it is sometimes urged that vocal melody having any claim to originality must become, by the mere cumulative exhaustion of possibilities, increasingly difficult to write. This may be true, though it is, to say the least, by no means certain that the more we know the less there is to know. Take, for example, the whole body of the Fugue subjects of Bach, than which there is not in music a more amazing array of significant melodic ideas. Are we to say that Bach has in any real sense narrowed the field of discovery ? Is it not more inherently probable that where one mind was able to extract so many crystals of melodic thought, there must be a vast remainder, could we but find them ? There is in this type of argument a radical fallacy on both sides. Bach did not invent his phrases. Every one of them had in detail been used hundreds

50

of times before. It was the imaginative relations in which he placed them that made them seem new. English poetry was not exhausted because Shakespeare covered almost the whole vocabulary of it. It is literally with those elements of an art that are most familiar that genius produces its most marvellous effects. We neglect vocal melody not because there is no more to be discovered, but because our interests and our talents lie elsewhere.

Granted, however, that an age will have originality at all costs, there are one or two obvious ways of accomplishing this, intellectual rather than imaginative though they may be. It is possible to exploit increasing angularities and to dwell on those intervals or phrases which appear to be comparatively new or strange. Here the price to be paid is formidable. It has been noted how deep and how exclusive are our intuitive melodic reactions. The composer who deliberately avoids them is rejecting just those factors of memory and association which constitute the infection of all artistic processes. This question will have to be discussed more fully with reference to extreme developments of contemporary texture. Here it need only be said that the essential æsthetic appeal of melody is something far more than its present statement. Every interval in it, every turn of phrase, either invokes or fails to invoke conscious or unconscious memories, and it is these memories and their associations which give the present sensation such completeness, satisfaction, or wealth of expression as it may have. The artist is playing on the accumulated intuitions of inheritance or education. Novel impressions are mere drops in this ocean. That experience will in time enlarge the vocabulary of thought is certain. But it is equally certain that each detail of advance is, with respect to the legacies of the past, a very small fragment. Substantial change in the fundamental reactions of the mind is a very gradual and a very slow process.

On the other hand, it must be admitted that lack of creative endowment carries with it a nemesis of equally devastating effect. Melody which is no more than a restatement of things that have been better said before will not for long deceive the listener. It is some such failure of sensitiveness which occasionally shocks us in Richard Strauss. When by all the standards of proportion the great tune should come, it is sometimes of a type that either repeats a familiar formula without distinction, or which gives it a conscious artifice that may sound gratuitously perverse. Some of the melodies of Strauss are at the same time too odd and too commonplace. The following is from *Don Quixote ;* it occurs at the most poignant moment of the story.

It is on account of these difficulties of association that many of the experiments now being made in unaccompanied song seem to be so lacking in æsthetic distinction. Three generations ago it was not unusual for a singer to be as happy without an accompaniment as with one, but the melodies so performed were of course of traditional type and form. The musical interest was inherent in the melody itself. Harmonies were either unnecessary or could be easily supplied imaginatively. The difficulty of introducing a convincing originality into an art so simple and so severe as this may be illustrated by an unaccompanied fragment from Wagner's *Tristan*

As pure melody this was too angular for his day, as indeed it is for ours. As implied harmony it is too

52

recondite. Hearers of average sensibilities need something much more reminiscent than this. Debussy succeeds better in *Pelléas* :

(31)

Mes longs cheveux descendent jusqu'au seuil de la tour;
Mes cheveux vous attendent tout le long de la tour;
Et tout le long du jour, Et tout le long du jour

Here there is no difficult interval or detail of phrase, no need for implied harmony. The singer is dealing with material towards which his physical reactions are technically attuned, a most important consideration in vocal production, and the listener finds the single line a serene and beautiful thing in itself. It is almost folk-music.

And this brings us to the middle path which has lately been explored with enthusiasm. The incorporation and imitation of folk-melodies, themselves relics of half-forgotten idioms, are common to many contemporary schools of thought. Associative elements are present which give these melodies a relation to experience, and some of their characteristic features are as yet refreshingly unspoiled by use. We are in fact beginning to take these old or old-fashioned ideas and use them somewhat in the manner of the old contrapuntists, who took fragments of plain-song, or melodies of less decorous antecedents, and used them as a pivot for decoration and texture. A new Council of Trent might be disposed to remove some of these old tunes from the attentions of the unscrupulous, but their effect in focussing interest on ideas of purely vocal origin is an asset of the highest value in the evolution of the melodic sense.

Such are some of the melodic and rhythmic problems of our day. So far as the incorporation of original ideas is concerned, it cannot be said that they have reached a stage which, in a general view, can be accepted as either coherent or stable. With regard to what we

hold to be the more important factor of pure melody·
when a composer will not versify, and when rhapsodic
development is outside his design, it is significant that
he often falls back on the practice of repeating scraps
of melody for just so long as their inherent interest,
or the clothes in which they can be dressed, will retain
a certain freshness. We emulate neither the flowing
streams of Bach, nor the carved panels of Mozart.
Many of the most beautiful and coherent works of
Debussy and Ravel, for example, are for the most part
mosaics composed of fragments which are undeniably
expressive, but which obey few of the traditional
principles of design. The Russians, and those of our
compatriots who imitate them or who think along lines
parallel to theirs, have carried the reiteration of melodic
fragments to an extreme degree. At the elaborate
dressing of these phrases our contemporaries are highly
skilled, and their harmonic costumes may change
almost from bar to bar. But considered primarily as
melody, and in relation to the evolution of melodic
forms, we are often very near to the most primitive
of all the ways in which a melodic idea can be stated,
that of simple repetition. Rob us of our texture, and
we are sometimes hardly to be distinguished from the
relics of an untutored art. This phenomenon need not
be further discussed. The reader acquainted with
contemporary work will recall numerous examples of
the manifold reiteration of little sections of melody,
sections which may be no more than the few notes
that constitute a quaint or novel turn of speech. At
best, these germs give us hopes of a better. At worst,
they raise again those problems of comparative value
which so harass the æsthetic appreciation of persistent
rhythms.

TEXTURE : THE EXPANSION OF TRADITION

'What was Greek music ? . . . I do not say that
they had no knowledge of harmony and part-writing,
but nobody, at all events, will deny that harmony and
part-writing amongst the Greeks were absolutely
rudimentary. . . . Are we then to say that the Greeks
in admiring their music showed bad taste, or are we
to say that our sensibility for musical excellence has
been so dulled by experience or by our natural in-
eptitude that we have got to apply to the means of
producing that emotion incomparably more labour,
. . . and that what we call the progress of music is
really the decrease in our musical sensibility ? '

A. J. Balfour : 'Questionings on Criticism and Beauty'.

OF the many formal characteristics which contemporary music exhibits, the most consistent
is its devotion to qualities of texture The
music which we immediately inherit had prevailing
interests of other kinds. The symphonic period busied
itself chiefly with problems of architecture. It had to
evolve, from the more or less versified dances of earlier
times, extended instrumental forms whose consistency
and cohesion had an architectural basis. The later
period of drama-in-music concentrated the essence of
its thought on the distillation of themes, whose function
was pivotal, and whose musical adventures in the body
of a work determined and justified its form. But though
there are to be found, among contemporary composers,
some who essay symphonic forms and who use thematic
values, modernity as a whole has deserted both the
practice of melodic versification, which was characteristic of even the greatest symphonic writers, and
the later cult which preferred thematic drama.

55

Contemporary music is predominantly a development of texture, and as the last great period in music when texture occupied this paramount place was that which is associated with Bach, it will provide an essential element of perspective if the two products are compared and contrasted. It is significant that modernity in this sense has synchronised with a growing appreciation of Bach.

The normal texture of Bach is contrapuntal, and its internal values have a horizontal derivation. He weaves melodic threads into a fabric whose quality is chiefly determined by the ordered beauty and individuality of its components. Harmonic values are also displayed, but these have their logical basis in the encounters of parallel strands of thought. The vertical splash of sound, so to speak, is not an end in itself. Chords seek their meaning in the behaviour of their parts. Tonality and form are equally contrapuntal in derivation, and must incorporate the general texture. Modulation, for instance, is not the mere handling of decisive chords; it is a detailed harnessing and guiding of individual parts, which may be disciplined in the process, but not destroyed.

Now a texture of this nature has its own ideals, its own limitations. It will demand, in the first place, the utmost cogency and beauty of melodic invention. It will equally insist on that economy and discipline of statement without which a brotherhood of melodies is impossible. And it will, above all, seek its climaxes in the intimacy and intensity of its thought, in the accumulated richness of its ordered complexity, rather than in the unexpectedness or vehemence of harmonic or dynamic contrasts. There are persistent rhythms in Bach, and there are arresting splashes of harmony, but they are usually complementary to his wealth of detail. They do not supplant it. And even the simplest harmonic or rhythmic framework can be richly clothed.

Compare these ideals with the values associated with our own day. Modern texture is normally vertical, harmonic, a fabric of splashes of sound. It indulges in what it is pleased to call polyphony, but a modern score has few real parts ; parts, that is, that have independent interest and validity for more than a short time. Orchestral parts now resemble horizontal sections cut through a landscape. They are like the contour lines of an ordnance map. They appear when the fabric reaches a particular degree of elevation. They disappear when the texture is thin. Their function in the technique is occasional, almost casual. Even where the musical apparatus is fairly constant, as in the string parts of an orchestra, or, indeed, in those of a quartet, there may be no real parts in the contrapuntal sense of the term. Everything is subject to vertical and harmonic exigencies, and modern players, with what our forefathers would have considered to be an amazing humility, have to be content with a place in the musical hierarchy which has just so little or just so much meaning as a composer-autocrat may determine. It is good if a part is interesting. It is no longer expected to be intelligible. Our values, in other words, are at right angles to those of Bach. We exploit masses and contrasts, and the medium is colour rather than line ; the fabric is wall-paper rather than tapestry. And the effectiveness of a contemporary composer's speech may depend almost exclusively on the sensitiveness or daring of his harmonic methods.

If this be considered an indictment of contemporary music, common fairness demands that it be not addressed solely, or even chiefly, to the composers of to-day. The mischief, if mischief it is, was done a century ago, and were Bach to return and survey the music which superseded his, it is not modernity in this sense that would first engage him. He would see that already in Haydn and Mozart the ' pretty tunes ' had won the day. Beautiful as it may be hoped he would find them to be, he could not overlook their essentially versified character. He would fear the danger of such rigid models, the temptation to lesser men to cultivate mere prettiness of melodic speech ; and the works of the minor composers of the nineteenth century would justify his misgiving. The grandeur of Beethoven's architecture would not make him blind to the dynamic vigour which was so important a constituent in his most characteristic works, a vigour which could and did encourage sheer vehemence in many who imitated him. And the harmonic texture reflected, while it was itself rendered still more crystalline by, these tendencies. Bach might point to the first chord of Beethoven's First Symphony (Ex. 33), to the first chord of the last movement of the Ninth (Ex. 34)—both of them examples of effects which arrest the attention by reason of unusual or forcible statement—and turning from these to the first chord of Scriabine's *Prometheus* (Ex. 35), he would find but a difference of degree.

Bach might be a little wistful when he reached the programme-musicians, for he was not averse to an occasional excursion into the realm of literal description. But he would undoubtedly agree that while external ideas may stimulate the fancy, they can also destroy the judgement, and they can never permanently replace the values of pure music. Finally, he would reach our humble selves. What have we to show him ? The pretty tunes are forsworn, the architecture is melting, the external dramas and labelled themes are a little out of fashion. One or two minor developments are new, at least in degree ; in particular, the wealth of local colours and of semi-barbaric rhythms. Asia and Africa are imported into the concert-room, and the drum is beaten harder than ever before. And there is one major development in the attention now concentrated on the traditional music of the people, an attention which certainly enlarges the melodic horizon, though it is as yet too often incongruously distorted by the trappings of a style centuries later in sophistication. These accretions apart, there remains of our inheritance a predominantly vertical texture, an ever-increasing apparatus of sound, and a consequent leaning towards harmonies and rhythms which are new, or rich, or strange.

The story of the century between Beethoven and ourselves may, therefore, from the point of view of texture, be fairly said to hinge on the exploitation of chords as such. Their relationships control the fabric, in which ' high lights ' take the form of exceptional combinations. In early stages comparatively mild forms arrest the attention. These are then greatly attenuated in effect by constant use. More striking values are discovered; and so on, *ad infinitum*. Examples from Beethoven have already been given. Chopin, Schumann, and, above all, Wagner, gave to this form of progress accumulating impetus. Even the initial crash of Mendelssohn's *Wedding March* embodied a popular taste already widely diffused.

It was essential to the function of such effects that they should be, in the technical sense, unprepared, and once this was granted, their use in like manner in the body of the work followed automatically. The use of chords striking in themselves or strange in their

59

context, and the unexpected inferences or ambiguities of tonality and texture that such use involved, became normal features in the technique of expression. And the degree to which this method was already latent may be seen in Beethoven himself (*Diabelli* Variations, No. 20).

The whole variation from which the above passage is taken is exceptional in many respects, but there can be no dispute as to its 'modernity', in the usual sense of that much-abused word. The vertical bias, the ambiguous tonalities, the chords. strange in themselves and still stranger in their context, are all present to an uncommon degree.

Compare with this a passage from Bach's *G minor Organ Fantasia* :

These passages should be studied in their context ; but exceptional as they are, both in their relation to the general texture of their respective composers, and in the convergence of style which, in isolation, they appear superficially to show, there is yet a clear difference of derivation. Bach rarely forgets his counterpoint. Beethoven rarely remembers his.

The jump to a texture typically modern is not very

formidable. The following is from Scriabine's *Poème de l'Extase*. It is reduced to essential terms :

The chord in bar 3 is a comparatively novel variation and inversion of the first chord in the passage, A natural being an appoggiatura on B flat. The tonal quality of this chord is ambiguous, as all whole-tone chords are, but it is resolved regularly, if a little elliptically, through bars 5 to 8.

A few bars later occurs the following, which is interesting because it involves an ambiguity of tonality comparable in some respects to Spohr's enharmonic mannerisms :

Two chords of the dominant seventh, an augmented fourth apart in pitch, have two notes in common, and it is possible to 'switch' from one to the other and back again indefinitely. Rimsky-Korsakov does this most effectively in *Schéhérazade:*

Ex. 39, above, incorporates the same device, more elaborately developed. Scriabine is very fond of it, and one could almost lay odds that when he reaches a

61

dominant chord of this kind he will move the root an augmented fourth, and it is then an even chance which tonality he will finally choose. It is the kind of device for which the chord of the diminished seventh became so notorious that our fathers could bear it no more. Richard Strauss has in our day, however, made this chord live again by using its ambiguity in a very condensed form. He moves the roots with great emphasis, and his result is at least so much stronger than Scriabine's in that Strauss has more roots to play with. See the *Symphonia Domestica* :

(41) *a*

The reader interested in the analysis of such effects should notice how the tied chord in Ex. 41*b* can be made to change its key-feeling kaleidoscopically by giving it in turn the various 'roots' which have been placed under it. It will be seen that Strauss's idiom involves three of these impressions.

Scriabine is in fact a formalist, and his most complex chords generally have classical foundations and resolve themselves more or less regularly at last. The following is from one of his piano pieces. The original is given, then a simplification, followed by the two resolutions which he alternately adopts. A second example of similar character is given verbatim :

(42)

The later Scriabine does not of course resolve in
traditional fashion chords so simple as the last one in
Ex. 43. The acceptance of such chords as final is a
tendency to be noted later. The formal element in
Scriabine's harmonic systems is his use of a chord of
classical derivation, made more complex by added
appoggiaturas, and elevated into a kind of anagram of
a whole movement. It is this that makes so much of
his music, once the novelty or the colour of it has worn
off, harmonically monotonous. There are not a few
of his works, many of them of substantial length, which
consist of nothing more than harmonic formulæ of
this kind, ingeniously exploited in themselves, and
clothed with a technical skill in other respects which
disgu ses for a time the essential narrowness of the
underlying structure. (See also Ex. 100.)

This much is obvious, however, that so far as chords
are built up on the traditional roots—thus, for instance :

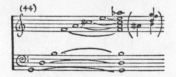

and used with whatever omissions or inversions, or with
it matters not how many superadded ' passing notes ',
as our fathers called them, or suspensions, or appoggiaturas, or what not : so far as they are thus built, and
subsequently resolved, directly or indirectly, in fair
consonance with inherited ideas of tonality, they are

in the direct line of classical descent. Their genealogy may be greatly condensed, but their behaviour betrays their parentage.

The break with tradition begins when such chords are either left in the air, or when they move in a manner that eliminates the classic inferences ; when they are unresolved, in fact. The end of the first act of *Pelléas et Mélisande* is an illuminating example in this regard :

(45)

The above passage is the end of an extreme diminuendo, and the sounds die away imperceptibly. Now the musician of a past generation would have demanded, and his imagination would probably have supplied, a resolution of the last chord analogous to the resolution which Debussy actually gives in the first bar quoted. It is possible to ' hear ' this imaginary resolution just as in moments of strained attention one can ' hear ' a pianissimo note on a violin for some time after the bow has ceased to touch the string. But with increasing familiarity the ear begins to dispense with such inferences, accepting Debussy's last chord as it stands as a point of rest, as a combination of notes already reduced to its simplest terms and having no necessary implications. And this chord may then become, as it actually has become in certain contemporary schools, invested with the finality, and incidentally with the monotony, that adheres to any conventional formula.

Another novel feature of Debussy's original style is what we may perhaps be allowed to call the harmonic 'side-slip'. He takes, for example, a chord of the ninth,

64

and slides away with it whole, in any direction, until whatever tonality it originally had is, to say the least, highly attenuated. It has simply left the classical track:

It should be noted that Debussy's originality lies in his choice of chords, rather than in his manner of using them. The mediaeval musician confronted with successions of chords of the sixth (Ex. 46 b) or of diminished sevenths (Ex. 46 c), such as have been accepted without comment for two centuries at least, would have felt a distressing lack of harmonic sense in the actual behaviour of the chords as such. The logic of these idioms is melodic rather than harmonic, and the only tribute they normally pay to intrinsic harmonic values is a fairly conventional relation between the first chord of a series and that which precedes it, and between the last chord and that which follows. In this respect Debussy is usually as orthodox as Beethoven or Bach.

These chords thus become 'points of rest', not so much because their normal inferences are discounted as because they cease, in such a context, to have any. It is then no more than a step to Goossens's:

The practice and extension of these methods cannot be adequately studied apart from their whole context in the texture, and this is beyond verbal treatment.

Quotation can give, at best, but a mere grammar of the subject. And grammatical inferences have a further disability which has to be constantly borne in mind. The composer himself may, and in many cases certainly will, deny that suggested elucidations of this nature have any real relation to the actual processes of his thought. He will use, for example, such progressions as the following (omitting the notes in brackets), and will affirm that his thought is absolutely direct from chord to chord :

But this does not deny to his hearer the right to discover historical foundations, conscious or unconscious, in the behaviour of such chords, and to interpolate imaginatively the inferences (in brackets) which traditionally belong to them and which may help to make an unfamiliar idiom clear. The composer is in this respect like the poet who chooses intuitively a word that may be magic in its effect. A commentator may legitimately analyse this effect into the associations which enrich the word in question. Our present purpose is commentary, and we conceive our danger to lie, not in the process of analysis, but in the inference that should above all things be avoided ; namely, that our laboured synthesis of detail has any conscious parallel in the inspiration of creative thought itself.

With this permanent reservation, the following passages from Delius's *Dance for Harpsichord* may be reduced to skeleton in order to show their bearing on the evolution of texture :

The last half-bar in Ex. 50 is a very clear case of the

contemporary tendency to eliminate what would heretofore have been considered the normal harmonic inferences. Delius's chord at the beginning of this last half-bar is identical with the last chord in Ex. 48 so far as the actual sounds are concerned. The originality of his thought consists in the way in which he sees the latent possibilities of such chords from an angle of vision which is at once more comprehensive and more subtle than that of tradition.

A very close and homogeneous texture of this kind is to be found in Ravel, and it is both illuminating and amusing to imagine the platitudes he did not utter Our quotation is from the *Valses nobles et sentimentales* The original is given first, and beside it a possible translation into musical journalese :

Another passage from the same work becomes a text-book exercise in suspensions and anticipations when the traditional resolutions are added, though it will be seen that many of these elements do move normally in Ravel's text itself, the disguise of their procedure lying in the simultaneous movement of other parts of the texture, which anticipates them and transforms them, when they do resolve, into further strange elements which may again resolve too late :

'Your grasp of the obvious is painfully precise', Ravel might say ; and the remark is just. But the present argument is so far fortified. A texture of this nature, however extreme in its condensation, yet has its logical foundation in classical traditions. Its novelty to our ears is due for the most part to its exclusive use of strong terms, its parallel avoidance of weak ones. Its obscurity, when it is obscure, may well be like that of classic verse, which is difficult rather through wealth of meaning than through lack of it.

More debatable ground is reached when traditional explanations are sought for passages such as the following from John Ireland's Prelude, *The Undertone.*

This passage shows forms of 'side-slip' analogous to those noted in Debussy and Delius. But is it legitimate to explain the connexion between the first two chords of the second bar by an ellipsis of thought which the note interpolated in brackets might fill, the B flat moving theoretically through B natural ? There must, of course, be a degree beyond which compression of thought ceases to be reasonably intelligible, though it would be dangerous to define such a limit. There are literary analogies. When Browning wrote :

> Who fished the murex up ?
> What porridge had John Keats ?

was he perversely obscure, or were his readers unexpectedly dull ? When we are told that the murex provided an ancient purple dye, a circumstance which to Browning carried an association with what are called purple patches in literature ; that writing of this ornate type was highly appreciated and rewarded in the case of men who had learnt the method from Keats ; and that Keats himself, the inventor of it, was allowed figuratively to starve ; when we know all this, then Browning's meaning is clear. But such compression is risking a great deal. Some have called it the compression of the telegraph-form. The way in which harmonic idioms can be condensed is open to exactly the same objection. The listener has to decide for himself when the thought is too compact to be communicable. Analysis may enlighten him intellectually, but it may not convince him æsthetically. And the composer on his part must be ready to admit at least a possibility of failure in this direction. It is not that the composer himself may not be able to think in comparatively cryptic terms. There is no doubt that he can and does. But the habit becomes dangerous when an impression is given, however unintentionally, that to be profound it is necessary to be abstruse. Then the imitators may flock together, and begin to say nothing with impressive obscurity.

TEXTURE : MULTIPLE TONALITY

Sir Toby : But shall we make the welkin dance
indeed ? Shall we rouse the night-owl in a catch that
will draw three souls out of one weaver ? Shall we do
that ?

Sir Andrew : An you love me, let's do't : I am a
dog at a catch. . . .

Malvolio : My masters, are you mad ? Have you
no wit, manners, nor honesty . . . that ye squeak out
your cozier's catches without any mitigation or re-
morse of voice ? Is there no respect of place, persons,
nor time, in you ?

Shakespeare : 'Twelfth Night'.

THE exploitation of masses of sound rather
than of threads of melody, and the consequent
tendency to seek expression as much in contrasts of quantity as in refinements of quality, were
consistent features in the music of the nineteenth
century. This is the music we inherit, and so far as
our own music is predominantly harmonic and dynamic
we may merit neither praise nor blame. It would,
however, be a serious omission on the part of an
observer if he were to accept these tendencies without question, neither inquiring into their origins, nor
asking whether the circumstances which engendered
or nourished them are or are not still prevalent.

The nineteenth century was a period of great material
expansion, and in this expansion music had a share.
At the beginning of the century it was mainly the
concern of the cultured few; at the end it had con-
formed to the democratic tinge which permeated the
whole society of Europe and America. The drawing-
room of a noble, the small theatre of a Court, the

assembly room of an exclusive circle, gave way to the public opera house and concert hall. The chamber-orchestra of Mozart became the concert-orchestra of Richard Strauss. Where Beethoven addressed hundreds, Wagner eventually addressed thousands, and it is not surprising that large and heterogeneous audiences should have encouraged vigorous and uncompromising speech. Of the multiplication of voices and instruments it is hardly necessary to speak. We play the clavichord-music of Bach on the modern grand piano, the symphonies of Mozart on the orchestra of Strauss. What is lost in delicacy is, perhaps, gained in breadth, and the incidental incongruities which are revealed in all processes of arrangement, whether conscious or unconscious, do not concern our immediate subject.

There are, however, certain material factors which appear to have had specific and definable effects on the actual texture of our music, and of these two may be taken as typical. They are both closely connected with the development and popularity of keyboard instruments; the first being a consequence of equal temperament in tuning, the second arising from the application of the keyboard to an instrument of markedly dynamic type.

Equal temperament made easy the use of extreme keys. That was its justification. The mediaeval modes were dead; music was, for better or worse, allied to systems of key relationships; and the widening of these relationships was the obvious path of advance. Extended movements were based on an architecture of keys, and incidental modulation was one of the most fertile methods whereby a composer could exhibit his command of technical resource, or exercise the vigour and originality of his fancy.

What then became of the so-called 'natural' instruments, instruments like the horn and trumpet, which were physical embodiments of one tonality, and of one only? All the wood-wind instruments had limitations

71

of a related kind. They were built in a particular key, and for a long time they had to be used with due regard to the mechanical difficulties which extreme modulation might create. The clarinet preferred from the first to be a transposing instrument, a change of instrument being the only alternative to the provision and manipulation of a very complex mechanism, a mechanism which could never be more than supplementary to the normal boring of a particular diatonic scale. It is true that horn and trumpet could play a first subject in C major and, after a short interval for a change of crook, could appear again in E flat or some other key. But the continuity of parts was lost irretrievably, and incidental modulations were inherently impossible. The most that could be done was to reinforce such arbitrary notes as happened to have an equivalent in the natural scale of the instrument, with an effect which was at best clumsy and at worst grotesque. The horn and trumpet parts of the classic symphonies are frequently of a type that had never before been admitted into the domain of serious music.

It is interesting to recall in this connexion the famous false entry of the horn in the first movement of the *Eroica* symphony (Ex. 54). Would it be too much to say that the very rigidity of the instrument, as it existed in his day, played a considerable part in Beethoven's inspiration ?

Thus Beethoven defied his limitations and endorsed a clash of tonalities ; and the success of so bold an experiment is, from the point of view of our own day, curiously prophetic.

The incisive tone of certain instruments needs special treatment. Some of them have great powers of emphasis. But in Bach's hands all instruments had to be melodious. There could be no barking and biting at notes which were devoid of logical sequence. And the dexterity with which the later symphonists dovetailed 'natural' instruments into an alien texture should not blind us to the arbitrariness of the whole process. All instruments became chromatic during the nineteenth century, but their earlier limitations remained for a long time embodied in a tradition that fed on the very disabilities from which great composers had suffered. When Beethoven modulated to a distant key he was compelled to leave part of his orchestra behind. When he returned, increased fullness of texture was unavoidably sudden. Effects of mass and of emphasis were thus fortified by classical practice, and continued to be unduly exploited long after their original justification had become obsolete. Even now too many musicians, creative and executive alike, appear to regard certain instruments and groups of instruments as primarily the vehicles of a kind of super-splash in the harmonic fabric. And the vehemence to which some instruments can be excited has been carried, by not a few composers of repute, to a point with which only an African drummer can compete.

This is one of our legacies. Another is the pianoforte. The piano would not be so omnipresent in the modern practice of music had it not offered substantial merits. Chief of these is the power it shares with all keyboard instruments of combining many parts in one performer. The pianist is himself a concert, in the literal sense of that word. To the complexities which the piano can suggest, and to the music which, to our ears at least, it will tolerably reproduce, there is practically no limit. The Elizabethans wrote music ' apt for voices or viols '. To us everything is ' apt ' for the piano. The discriminating may protest, but the broad fact remains.

Yet the piano has at least three major limitations. It is an instrument of percussion, it is confined to a hand-technique, and it is intonation-proof. Melody on the piano is akin to melody on kettledrums, to melody on bells. The piano is a mechanical dulcimer. Apart from the actual noise of the hammer-blows, obvious on a bad instrument and by no means inaudible on a good one, the melodic power of the piano is of a very peculiar kind. Every note is an explosion, followed by a rapidly failing vibration. We can discount the noise as we can discount the scratch of a gramophone. We reinforce imaginatively the failing vibrations. But the instrument retains none the less its fundamentally dynamic quality. Throughout early history serious music was an affair of the voice, or of instruments which aspired to be vocal, whether bowed or blown. The primitive harp, and still more the primitive drum, had no part in the growth of music from melody to polyphony. This polyphony, representing the golden fruit of centuries of labour, was applied to the key-board. With the keyboard it fought an heroic but unquestionably a losing battle. There was no help for it. The keyboard had come to stay, and many of the instruments to which it was allied were negations of all that polyphony had hitherto implied. We still pay the old music tribute, for our minds idealise the graduated but none the less clumsy explosions of the piano into memories of the sustained melody which to most of us is the essence of music. But the ubiquity of a dynamic keyboard cannot be without serious re-actions on standards of texture, and it is not merely fortuitous that the century which adopted the piano adopted also an increasingly quantitative idea of values.

The hand-technique of the piano is, whether good or bad, inevitable. All instruments have such limita-tions, and it is within them that an art wins its spurs. But in this respect also the piano thrives on chords,

74

not on counterpoint. The playing of true polyphony is very difficult, and the result often ambiguous at best. Chords are only too easy, within the compass of the hand. And it is a commonplace of criticism that the piano classics are full of crude splashes of hand-music as raw and ugly as anything in the whole history of technique. A thick splash in the bass combined with a thin splash at a remote distance in the treble—this was an accepted formula. (See the reduction given in Ex. 57 below, which omits an accompaniment of close arpeggios, all within the octave first given in the bass). Beethoven's clumsiness is forgotten in the grandeur of his ideas, but the music of lesser men may come too often from the hand rather than from the head. The endless octaves of the piano, in particular, are devices of emphasis as barren artistically as anything music can show.

(55) 8va.....   (56)

Exs. 55 and 56 give two contemporary specimens which it is impossible not to regard as 'hand-music'. Such things may be justified to some extent in their context, but when the characteristic hops and skips of the piano, and the arpeggios which are properly fitting to it, are incongruously imported into other spheres— and they are not unknown even in music which presumably aspires to be sung—then it is time to open one's ears.

A third characteristic of keyboard instruments is perhaps most significant of all. They are peculiarly suited to the tone-deaf. The notes are ready made. All that is required of the performer is sufficient mental and physical agility to make eye and hand follow the

75

notation. The ear has no essential function in the production of the notes, and all the other processes involved can be tolerably executed by a mechanical player. From this follow two important reactions.

In the first place, whatever combinations of notes can be imagined, whatever can be written down, can be reproduced in essentials without further difficulty. The writer does not have to rely exclusively on the accuracy of his aural imagination, or wait until singers or players can be found who are able and willing to produce the combinations he desires. The composer's mind is still, of course, the true creative medium ; but the piano offers him an ideal field for experiment. By its means he can cultivate his harmonic sense to a very high degree, breaking as much new ground in a year as his fathers did in a century. And in like fashion those who would follow the processes of his thought can learn quickly by means of the piano to tolerate or to enjoy dissonances and complexities which a lifetime of purely orchestral or choral experience might not render familiar to the same extent. Take the chord Ex. 56 above. It is easy to play on the piano as it stands, in isolation. To reproduce it chorally on the same terms would require ten singers, each gifted with absolute pitch and uncommon powers of concentration. Failing such endowments, the singers would have to approach the chord by means of ten separate melodies, every one of which would have to display sufficient coherence to enable the singer to grasp and hold his particular strand of the fabric. This was the contrapuntal method, the vocal method—may one say the musical method ? It was the method that the keyboard could dispense with.

Secondly, and to the same degree, keyboard music, so far as it is unvocal, demands from the singer or orchestral player, whose province it invades, precisely that automatic and mechanical intonation which the keyboard provides. All cultivated singers and stringed or wind instrument players complain that contemporary

76

music is too frequently of a type utterly foreign to their particular medium. They have been educated to make their own notes, to appreciate niceties of intonation and quality; to be, in fact, intelligent interpreters of an intelligible part. When they are asked to behave like automata, they are docile perhaps, but none the less bewildered. And this attitude goes deeper than the mere question of technique. Such music often finds capable performers. The pity is that it so rarely leaves them inspired.

Considerations such as have been thus briefly indicated are directly related both to characteristic features in contemporary music and to the pace at which they have developed. Should the twentieth century do no more than consolidate the ground it has already explored, it would still show a marked originality. Yet many of its tendencies were at least latent in its predecessors, and so far as the complexity and condensation of harmonic idiom is concerned, to-day is but the child of yesterday. Can the same be said of all our experiments ? Is there a classical justification for our deliberate multiplication and confusion of tonalities, for instance ; for chords of which one-half is frankly A major, and the other half just as frankly E flat minor ?

Ex. 54 above is very exceptional, but there is one classical device which does occur frequently and which implies at least a partial confusion of keys. This is the use of pedal-points. The pedal-point is presumably descended from the drone of certain primitive instruments. It is found in every kind of music from the very earliest times, and since our key system became fixed its function has been quite clearly that of preserving the atmosphere of a particular key in spite of the modifications or modulations that might occur in the harmonic superstructure. And this process logically involves a clash of tonalities. The following examples are typical. Numerous examples in Bach will also occur

77

to the reader, though these are generally less modern in feeling because their texture is more contrapuntal. The modern method is uncompromisingly harmonic.

Ex. 57 is from Beethoven's Opus 110. It is bold, but orthodox. Ex. 58 is condensed from the second act of *Parsifal*. It begins classically, but becomes increasingly ambiguous. Ex. 59 is from Elgar's *Cockaigne.* It has the modern bluntness of speech, and it illustrates incidentally that rigidity of style which has already been noticed as belonging to 'natural' brass instruments. Ex. 60 is a mere fragment of the long dominant pedal with which Richard Strauss closes Variation X of *Don Quixote.* The reader should study the whole passage as it occurs in the work. It may fairly be said to represent the greatest complexity which this classical device had reached by the end of the last century.

It will be noticed that not only do the dissonances become more acute in the later examples, but that the composer is more and more inclined to emphasise them, to dwell on them, to make the clashes of tonality undisguised. Chords like that in the last bar of Ex. 60 may, so long as they are held unresolved, be made the foundations of extended passages in which two clearly defined keys are simultaneously emphasised and exploited. Thus multiple tonality in a comparatively extreme form may be closely linked with classical tradition.

But it is a commonplace of musical history that the preparation and resolution of discords are never more than temporary dilutions of statement. Composers and public alike will drink their wine neat at the earliest possible moment. And there is no increase of incidental complexity that will not sooner or later dispense with the logical process that first gave it birth, and arrogate to itself an independent and intrinsic value. The chord we have just referred to is a typical case: it should resolve classically as in Ex. 61 (*a*), and so it does resolve eventually in *Don Quixote*. Ex. 61 (*b*) shows a little further complication, yet it also resolves classically as stated.

(61) *a*

But Ex. 61 (*b*) gives us A major plus E flat minor Why disguise the fact ? Why seek to minimise the effect of it by preparation or resolution or other temporary palliative ? Strauss, by the time he reached *Elektra*, had made the kind of step that all musicians

79

are constantly making throughout their experience. He had learnt to leave out everything which to him was inessential, and he writes bluntly:

The chord in Ex. 61 (a) has become remarkably popular as a vehicle for effects of ambiguous tonality, and it repays analysis. The elements of it occur in countless passages, of which the following, transposed from Bach, is one that also shows a characteristic use of a pedal-point.

Note in Ex. 63 (a) chords three and four. In the text-books they occur as in Ex. 63 (b). The first is a 'Neapolitan' sixth, the second one of its condensed resolutions. Strauss 'telescoped' them as in Ex. 63 (c). And below are given a few contemporary statements of the same idiom.

They are taken from Holst: *Hymn of Jesus* (64), Ravel: *Jeux d'Eaux* (65), and Stravinsky: *Pétrouchka* (66).

Stravinsky has no hesitation in using such harmonic

80

syntheses in their most bare and striking form. Thus
he also writes in *Pétrouchka* :

Ex. 67 is played by two solo clarinets at a moment
of intensity in the action. Ex. 68 is given to two bassoons
and is presumably comic. But the path from the
sublime to the ridiculous is of the same diminutive
length, whether measured forwards or backwards ; and
a truth may begin in jest. Thus Bartòk can write quietly
and lyrically :

The tonal ambiguity that can be extracted from
many of the chords discussed in the preceding chapter,
chords classically derived but involving great harmonic
complexity, needs no demonstration. It will be sufficient to note, as an exceptional case, the telescoping of
major into minor. The method condenses Schubert's
beautiful alternations, through Strauss's expressive
' false relations ' Ex. 70 is from the *Symphonia
Domestica*), into Stravinsky's final word on the subject.
Ex. 71 is from *Le Sacre du Printemps*.

The derivations already given explain historically a few of the complications of tonality which are now current, but there is another method of approach, at once more original, more fertile, and more promising, which deserves close attention. It may perhaps be defined approximately as the evolution of harmonic counterpoint. The conflict of styles, harmonic as against contrapuntal, which occupies so central a position in the history of music, and the final result of which was to all appearances the victory of the former, has reached a new phase, a phase which may be destined to incorporate both harmony and counterpoint in an inclusive whole. An example from Strauss's *Salome* will make the definition clear :

The theme in the upper stave of Ex. 72 suggests a simple diatonic harmonisation. It is thus treated in various forms earlier in the work. But at a moment of crisis in the drama Strauss ' harmonises ' it by means of the chords given below it. The theme still retains its diatonic character, and its thirds practically define simple harmonies. Meanwhile the accompaniment moves to a point outside the diatonic atmosphere and at the moment of separation (*) we are given a glimpse of what were at that time new and strange lands. The impression is the more vivid in that both streams of harmony meet again at once, and the vision dissolves as it arose. This is harmonic counterpoint. The melodic threads of the contrapuntist have become composite streams of harmony, and these streams may approach and recede, coalesce or clash, just as did the individual parts of polyphony.

82

The evolution of this texture has obvious analogies with the tentative experiments that elaborated organum from plain-song, and counterpoint from organum. The tenth century wrote :

The twentieth century writes :

To Otger, or Hucbald, or whoever wrote *Musica Enchiriadis*, Ex. 73 was a combination of two melodies, Ex. 74 of three. From the point of view of the development we are now discussing, and ignoring for the time being the pedal-points which here as elsewhere act as a kind of north-star to the adventurous composer, Exs. 75 and 76 (Debussy: *La Cathédrale engloutie*, and Holst: *The Planets*: 'Mars') represent single strands of thought. The curiously intimate relation of these typical passages to various technical factors is very significant. They frankly 'side-slip' in any required direction, and although the sound-medium for which they are written may be either a single keyboard or a combination of soloists, it is difficult to avoid the thought that for

83

harmonies which thus slide about in blocks the hand
of the pianist or organist is an ideal agent.

We have two hands, and even if we had not, it could
not long have escaped the notice of our inventive
century that harmonic streams of this kind might well
be combined. And it is in precisely this fashion that
some forms of multiple tonality first find expression.
A delightful example occurs in Stravinsky's *Pétrouchka*:
Ex. 77. It is diatonic, like Debussy's Ex. 75 above, and
this gives its incidental combinations a flavour which is
perhaps as much modal as multiple. But it is easy to
see how violent the impacts of such contending masses
could be made.

Stravinsky did not invent the method. It can be
found in essentials in passages from the works of other
and older composers. Strauss, in particular, frequently
organised passing effects of this kind. There are suggestions of it at the end of Ex. 72 above, and for a
thoroughly daring exploitation of chords moving in
oblique or parallel blocks, the reader may be referred
to the Battle-section of *Ein Heldenleben*, a work written
in the 'nineties. What distinguishes the twentieth
century is its increasing ruthlessness. Strauss would
often make detailed modifications in his chord-streams
in order to bring the total effect within a comparatively
respectful distance of what used to be called harmony.
Our contemporaries have no such reservations. The
harmonic columns march boldly on their way, and
they ignore or defy traditional good manners just as
the early pioneers of counterpoint did. The latter
shattered the select hierarchy of consonant intervals
by promoting thirds and sixths. Our young reformers
84

bombard the citadels of the classics with a shrapnel of dismembered keys. The motto of both revolutions is the same : 'Ça ira'.

Ex. 78 is from Holst's *Hymn of Jesus*. It is a daring and at the same time a highly successful example of choral exploration. The parts begin consonantly and end consonantly, and they can therefore be sung accurately. Ex. 79 is from one of Goossens's piano pieces.

But there is one major restriction which is common to all the examples just quoted. Their constituent streams consist exclusively of common chords. Why should the method be thus cabined and confined ? There is no logical reason, and a mind that has travelled thus far will not hesitate to take the next step and use other and more complex chords in the same way. The following is typical of a texture used freely by Goossens and others :

The stages by which a certain degree of finality may eventually be reached are clearly outl.ned in one of the sections in Stravinsky's *Le Sacre du Printemps*. Ex. 81 may be called the 'key' of the section. The bass is constant throughout. Ex. 82 shows a simple diatonic tune presented in parallel strands which form harmonies to which Ex. 81 is the key. This is the first superstructure. Ex. 83 adds a third and internal 'harmonic counterpoint', which is curious in itself, and against which the other elements are remorselessly driven without the slightest apparent regard for traditional euphony.

It is difficult to account for so deliberate a choice and so crude a use of extreme intervals, except on the ground of sheer harmonic satiety. Successions of major sevenths, such as are found in Stravinsky's internal accompaniment above, are already becoming in certain circumstances a kind of *cliché* fairly comparable to the consecutive fifths and fourths of organum. Major sevenths are tonally ambiguous, and are therefore strong meat. But philosophers are agreed that, dull as eternal bread and butter may be, eternal plum cake is worse.

As thus practised, is not the whole method clearly Hucbaldian in its present stage of development ? Out of it may come technical means as fertile in beauty as those of classical polyphony. But it may fairly be said

that this consummation is not yet. How far it is
' devoutly to be wished ' will depend on the gifts that
posterity may bestow on it.

Just as chords built on traditional foundations became in time conventionalised and accepted as ' points
of rest ', so, too, the chords evolved by incidental clashes
of tonality are now frequently used without further
elucidation. A passage from Goossens's choral work,
Silence, shows this development of technique in a comparatively mild form. Note that old and well-proved
sheet-anchor, the pedal.

But movements can now begin with chords like the
following (Ex. 85 is from Goossens's *Nature Poems*, Ex.
86 from Stravinsky's *Three Pieces for String Quartet*),
and the reader will have no difficulty in finding, in
works of this type, chords of every degree of ambiguity
and complexity used without the slightest attempt to
incorporate the old-fashioned logic of preparation or
sequence.

A passage in which conflicting tonalities are thus
bluntly combined forms a striking feature of the
' Neptune ' movement in Holst's *The Planets*. It is
interesting musically, but it is perhaps still more interesting psychologically. The movement suggests an
atmosphere strange, nebulous, and remote, and the means

87

employed is the alternation and combination of the two keys of E minor and G sharp minor. The following is a reduced version of the salient theme :

Technically the movement is masterly, as Holst almost invariably is, in that the effect produced is clearly and exactly that which the composer had in mind. Psychologically it is remarkable because of its intimate relation to a cognate effect, sought by Wagner in the theme of the *Tarnhelm :*

Both composers desire an atmosphere of mystery. Both use the same two keys. Expand and combine Wagner's alternating tonalities, and the product is Holst. Holst had, of course, no conscious thought of Wagner in mind either when he chose these particular chords or when his imagination ' telescoped ' them. And this is clear proof, if proof were needed, that what appear to be most daring and original ideas are normally but the latest fruits of a particular heritage.

The end towards which these developments are converging is a field of speculation which to some degree concerns all who practise or explore the art of music. Multiple tonality must, in the last analysis, mean no tonality at all, in the accepted sense of that term. No tonality, in the present state of our musical apparatus, leads to pure chromaticism. And pure chromaticism can only be logically defined as a technique in which the chromatic scale alone has fundamental validity, all intervals within it and all chords derived from it being theoretically of equal consonance. Contemporary music has not blanched at this prospect, and we must face the discussion of it. This discussion will raise, in an acute form, questions which underlie all æsthetic judgements. An art without conventions, without forms, or without limits is to that extent an art without values. Can an art without values be properly considered an art at all?

NOTE.—Since these chapters were written, I have come across a reference to the views of Beethoven's contemporaries which I cannot forbear to quote. The following sentences occur in a defence of Beethoven published in the *Musical World* dated March 25, 1836. H. J. Gauntlett wrote the article, and the italics are his.

' Beethoven also mystified his passages by a new treatment of the resolution of discords, which can only be described in words by the term, *resolution by ellipsis*, or the omission of the chord upon which the discordant notes should descend. . . . Many of his passages also appear confused and unintelligible, by a singular freedom in the use of diatonic discords or discords of transition ; many instances appear of passages by contrary motion, each carrying their harmonies with them. In the obstinate manner in which he drives one passage through and against another, he has no equal, except *Sebastian Bach* and our illustrious countryman *Samuel Wesley* Lastly, he produces the most mysterious effects, by the use of the *point d'orgue* [pedal-point] and its inversions.'

TEXTURE : CHROMATICISM

Hippolyta : This is the silliest stuff that ever I heard.

Theseus : The best in this kind are but shadows, and the worst are no worse, if imagination amend them.

Shakespeare : ' A Midsummer-Night's Dream'

DEVELOPMENTS of technique normally have their origin in the driving power of the imagination. The composer is impelled to engage in a search for means of expression. These means must be fitting and adequate to his ideas. If his ideas are markedly original, the expression of them is likely to demand a similar distinction of technique. The conscious elaboration of a technique is, of course, a highly intellectual process, and the intellect may so far anticipate or dwarf the imagination as to indulge in experimental novelties that are as yet only partially assimilated in the prevailing tone of the composer's mind. The balance between creative fancy and executive power is extremely delicate, and its disturbance is responsible for most of the failures and flaws that mar the practice of an art. *Kapellmeistermusik*—music, that is, which rehearses without particular distinction the familiar lines of a classical model—is a common form of intellectual bias. Excess of imagination, on the other hand, may make an artist the victim, rather than the master, of his ideas. Granted, however, that imaginative power is the first essential, it is tempting to ask what apparatus of expression a composer might ideally demand. He cannot create a new earth. He is himself the product of impressions that come to him initially from without. But his fancy can and does combine the features of his peculiar sensitiveness into new associations, and the

90

technical instrument suited to their expression would incorporate a corresponding wealth of resource.

He may, for example, legitimately idealise every known variety of tone-colour, every degree of significant force, and this throughout the whole range of his sensitiveness to pitch. The Bass Flute is not, in his mind, either a rare or a restricted instrument. His imaginative medium is the perfect orchestra and the perfect choir in one. He is also conscious of all those niceties of expression which defy notation. The *glissando* of a string, the *portamento* of a voice, the subtlety of an intonation that is sharp and bright, or flat and dull, as may be ; the delicate variations of time and rhythm, without which there is no flexibility of atmosphere ; all these may be vivid realities in the imaginative ear. Compare them with the severe and intractable limitations within which the composer's ideas have somehow to find external utterance, and it is not difficult to understand why he so often hovers on the verge of the impossible.

The practical deficiencies of voices and instruments, whether natural or arbitrary, cannot be catalogued. They are innumerable. The rhythmic tyranny involved in a complex *ensemble*, and the anarchy of detail which is the other extreme—these are the Scylla and Charybdis between which the composer's ship distressfully labours. Even the simplest course may strike the uncontrollable vagaries of a solo interpreter. Nor is this all. A limitation of the most fundamental kind has been imposed on all the music of our civilisation by the adoption of a particular system of intervals. Of the infinite number of notes which can be produced within the octave of voice or string, there are now only twelve that are orthodox. Keyboard and notation have conspired to ordain that these twelve notes, and no others, shall be music. There is still within us a vestige of independence that may express itself in varieties of intonation, but our notation ignores them, and our keyboards have flatly and finally decided that they shall not exist. Twelve notes, however, are at least twelve notes, so long as they can be used with consistent freedom. Within them something more comprehensive than we have yet experienced might conceivably be said. But we are not allowed even this. Classical tradition has concentrated the weight of its authority on the universal adoption of two particular and closely related chains of seven of these twelve notes. Compared with the varieties of combination, melodic or harmonic, which unlimited chromaticism seems to offer, the major-minor system is a convention of intolerable narrowness. Yet every melody that is classic, every chord, every modulation, every form, is bound by one of these two formulæ, each of which is no more than a comparatively slight modification of the other The accumulated inertia of them is enormous. To defy them is to defy Bach and Beethoven and all the composers whose immediate heirs we are. Three centuries of expansion, both formal and material, have but driven them deeper into the foundations of our thought, and they have become exalted in our minds to a position comparable with that of the fundamental axioms of science. If the geometry of Euclid be not real, and uniquely real, then we know very little about reality. If the harmonic system of Bach and Beethoven be not music, and uniquely music, then we know very little about music. Such are the constraints to which the inspiration of the contemporary composer is subject. It is just conceivable that he may shatter some of them.

All the advances in complexity of texture which may properly be called evolutionary have accepted the classical harmonic system as more or less axiomatic. Music of this kind has elaborated the argument, but it has not seriously challenged the premisses. The growth of multiple tonality has also involved at least a lip-service to the old values, and its detail has preserved

92

many traditional elements. In both these developments it is the mixture that is new, not the ingredients.

The conscious approach to what we propose to call pure chromaticism* is a tendency of a different kind. It is an attack on the foundations of texture, and the reader will have already guessed the direction from which the assault is being delivered. The elaboration of the classical key-system can be carried to a point at which every note in the chromatic scale is involved, and this is a form of chromaticism complete to a degree. In the same way, as has already been remarked, multiple tonality logically involves all possible combinations of tonalities, and this again is a form of chromaticism. But both these tendencies have inherent values which are derived from conventions of the traditional kind. They involve many dimensions, so to speak, but all these dimensions are Euclidean. It is a change in the fundamental logic of texture which distinguishes a third and further development. In certain details its product may not appear to differ greatly from extreme forms of the other tendencies. There is, however, a profound difference of derivation, and this carries with it a commensurate change of values. Pure chromaticism would ignore the whole hierarchy of historical

---

* The word *atonality* has recently been used to describe, presumably, developments which I prefer to define as modal, neomodal, or chromatic, respectively. My difficulty is that I cannot find a logical definition of atonality. If tonality means, as it surely does for most of us, the classical key-system, does atonality mean mere absence of this? Does it, therefore, include the old modes as well as the new, or the one, or the other, or neither? Does it cover the whole-tone scale? If it includes all this it is useless for purposes of exact description. If its range is narrower than this, then what is taken from it becomes attached, logically, to tonality. I see no escape from this ambiguity, which is the worst fault a technical term can have. Chromaticism, on the other hand, is a well-known and consistent historical tendency towards scalar expansion. The various stages in its progress are represented by the fixed scales to which music has from time to time attached itself. The end towards which all expansions logically converge is pure chromaticism, as defined in the text.

associations. It would dethrone all particular scales, for example, as having no more than relative purport. And the system to which these subsidiary values would be subject is the undiluted chromatic scale itself. The whole twelve notes are demanded, not in any order of precedence, not with any real or imagined grades of dissonance, but as a homogeneous medium in which all intervals, all scales, and all chords have equal prescriptive validity.

The desire for some such radical reform was stated with characteristic vigour in Busoni's pamphlet, *Entwurf einer neuen Aesthetik der Tonkunst* (Berlin, 1907). Busoni has been the champion of some of the most daring exponents of reform, and his views demand attention. He wanders into suggestions for elaborating the chromatic scale itself. He would divide each whole-tone into six parts, leaving the semitone (three-sixths) intact, but offering additionally third-tones and sixth-tones to the vocabulary of the future. With this scheme it is not necessary to deal. It is but one of many expansions which have from time to time been suggested. They are easy to devise, and so far as they make us realise that our chromatic scale is probably little more than a historical accident, they encourage an attitude of humility which is good for the soul. But they are not practical politics. The chromatic scale is fortified by the material apparatus, not to mention the living traditions, of our music, and it is inside this limit that reform, if reform be needed, must first come. On this narrower but more practical ground complaint is made of the rigidity and arbitrariness of the major-minor system, of its monopoly of melody, harmony, and form, and of the virtual extinction of all alternatives. Busoni asks us to observe the characteristic and novel flavour of a scale such as the following :

(89)

We are to think of C as the first and final note, the
tonic, in fact, of the scale. Busoni makes no suggestion
as to whether there is to be a dominant (fixing the key,
or mode, if any), or other internal values which might
have precise significance. So far, indeed, we are at the
stage of an incipient mode, in the mediaeval sense, but
without any of the internal relations which the middle
ages discovered and organised, and by means of which
modal melody, harmony, and form grew into being.
There will be more to say on this point later.

Busoni goes on to suggest that we should try this
scale (it is presented as a type, not as having peculiar
importance) in combination with various tonalities,
thus :

(90)

Further, we are to reflect on the possibilities of melodic
and harmonic expansion offered by a whole galaxy of
new scales, of which the following are a few :

(91)

Every scale so formed—and Busoni puts the number of
recognisably unique scales, including those already in
use, at one hundred and thirteen—undoubtedly has
its own peculiar flavour, and if these characteristic
features could be made the basis of so many melodic
and harmonic systems, it is no over-statement to hold,
as Busoni does, that even at a first glance there is a
prospect new and open, a certainty of immense discovery, and a contingent expansion of artistic material

95

in comparison with which the classical system is but an instrument of one string*.

It will be well perhaps at this point to deal with objections on the score of dissonance, objections which are perennially raised but which never have any apparent effect on practice. Let us admit at once that the attempt to find a consistent physical or mathematical basis for our impressions of consonance breaks down hopelessly. Of a few simple intervals, carefully adjusted, it may be said that they have mathematical affinities. Ratios of vibration alone, however, will not account for the consonance to our ears of any of the harmonic systems actually in use. In primitive times physical simplicity may have had some slight connexion with the intuitive choice of intervals, but it must be remembered that music was in the first place melody, not harmony, and what was initially sought was melodic distinctness. Primitive music—and our own was no exception to this rule—hardly conceives of the possibility of using various notes simultaneously. There was certainly no notion of ordered relations of this kind when our own melodic intervals were first explored. And it is probably this radical confusion of purpose that has made every attempt to derive harmony from mathematics, rather than from melody, a fruitless and perplexing task. The octave is more consonant than the semitone, but it was just those intervals which are nearest to mathematical purity, octave, fifth and fourth, that first became artistically barren. It is the ambiguous thirds and sixths that now play the chief part in our ideas of euphony. The whole system is a convention,

* The *scala enigmatica* which Verdi uses as a *canto fermo* in his *Ave Maria* (1898) is apparently a tentative exploration of one of these possibilities. Verdi's scale consists of the notes C, D flat, E, F sharp, G sharp, A sharp, B and C ascending, and of C, B, A sharp, G sharp, F natural, E, D flat and C descending. His harmonies are daring in their enharmonic devices and ambiguities, but their structure and behaviour are broadly consonant with traditional values.

and there is no reason to suppose that it is any more final than its predecessors. Equal temperament must have been excruciatingly painful to the hyper-sensitive, but the immediate wealth of melodic and harmonic expansion that it offered overcame all opposition. Beauty in this matter is in the ear of the listener. It is an acquired taste, not an intuitive reaction.

To return to Busoni. There are two important qualifications which must be observed when attempts are made to enlarge the vocabulary of music from this angle. In the first place a scale is not music, in the sense that music is an art. A scale is an intellectual abstraction. It is a formula derived from the analysis of melody. The creation of melody involves all the conscious or unconscious processes of the imagination, all the subtle and indefinable associations of memory and fancy, past and present. These it precipitates into significant relations, and it is these relations which are melody, which are music. The scale that can be extracted from this product is what remains when all the music has been taken away. To say, therefore, that a new scale, derived from an intellectual or arbitrary source, offers a field for musical expansion, is to state a hypothesis rather than a truth. Such a scale may indeed suggest to the sensitive imagination new relations, but it is only after the imagination has done its work, associating these new elements with the stored experiences of the mind and so fixing their relative significance, that they can become, even for the creator himself, vehicles of artistic expression. And this is not enough. The hearer must have the same sense of values, or a capacity for experience that will enable him to evolve them, or the new dialect is meaningless. This lack of parallel experience is naturally a marked feature in a heterogeneous musical public. To many men the music of some of their contemporaries is quite literally ' full of sound and fury, signifying nothing '. That the public may be ignorant, or the composer mad, merely accentuates the difficulty. Even the profoundest thinker must write in a language that a reader can read. Let all the nouns on this printed page be taken to represent a new and unfamiliar kind of preposition ; that will provide a fair literary parallel to the unassimilated values of a new scale.

And the second qualification is a particular application of the first. It is refreshing to find that we are to taste the flavour of these new scales with reference to chords of C major, A minor, and the like. We are to try them, in fact, with something we know, relate them, if we can, to the harmonic system we have inherited. This is the kernel of the whole matter. It is precisely in these and similar relations that the whole meaning of music consists. Without them there is no music. Every scale, qua scale, is in isolation arbitrary and meaningless. Every note, interval, or chord is in the same plight. These elements have significance only in their relations, and these relations are for most of us, whether we like it or not, the traditional values of the classics. It is futile to tilt, for example, at a common chord as such. It may be, historically, an accident, out of tune, illogical to any degree. Logic of this kind has nothing to do with music. The sound of a common chord has typified, throughout the evolution of the music that is nearest to us, a relative sense of finality, of repose, of balance, of perfection, of a score of other analogous states of mind. These are its meaning, both technically and psychologically, and the composer who avoids it simply does not and cannot say just these things. He may, and no doubt will, in time, invest with similar associations other forms of expression. It is in the slow growth and change of these associations that the panorama of artistic history consists. But until the change is effected, until the new formula has gathered to itself all the associations which belonged to its predecessors—until then it will, so far as certainty and intensity of effect are concerned, compete

98

hopelessly with the old. This is why mere novelty is so
empty, and why true creative power, be it never so
masterly and sincere, has to struggle hard for recog-
nition. The classics provide the background for all our
experiments. They therefore exact the respect that so
elemental a function requires.

An examination of the way in which chromaticism,
in the sense defined, influences the texture of music
may very well begin with Beethoven. The reader will
remember a characteristic audacity in the last movement
of the Eighth Symphony.

This is the Beethoven touch : a long and orthodox
preparation of the dominant C, ending in a sudden
and violent C sharp. Return is made at once to the
key of the movement, and the point to be noticed is
that, so far, the meaning of the C sharp is hardly more
than that it is not C ; it is as ' not-C ', so to speak, as
Beethoven could make it. The vocabulary is enlarged
by a new word, but the word is strange, hardly more than
an expletive, as thus presented. Later, another journey
is made over the same ground. When the famous C
sharp is reached, however, there is a marked expansion
of statement.

Eventually the normal key again returns, but in the
meantime the C sharp has become very much more than
' not-C '. It has found relations, not to other notes alone,

but to characteristic harmonies, to things redolent of the whole movement. It has become an integral part of the fabric. So do new words grow into a language.

That this classical language was international was a prime factor in its consolidation. The classics rarely distract us with ideas of locality. There are features which we discriminate in this way, as when we speak of German, French, or Italian influences. But these divisions, even at their keenest, are very slight when compared with the foundations common to them all. Scale, harmony, and form were essentially homogeneous throughout cultivated music, and developments of texture, wherever practised, had a closely parallel evolution. Beethoven had little to fear in the literary, political, or racial divisions of Europe, nor could the growth of nationalism, which was so pronounced in the nineteenth century, destroy this essential identity of experience. The native cast of Chopin, for example, did no more than give to his music an accent that might be traced to Polish sources. His speech was cosmopolitan. In the same way Dvořàk, Grieg, the earlier Russians, and others have since spoken in tones that had in them something akin to the atmosphere of a dialect. But these characteristics were never more than just sufficient to flavour the product, and a broad acceptance of classical values gave a setting to that discreet piquancy which captivated all societies while alienating none. They succeeded or failed, as the case might be, by reference to traditional standards. What has distinguished the late nineteenth and the early twentieth centuries is a deliberate exaggeration of dialects or mannerisms of this kind, and there are numerous examples which appear to assert that a pronounced local accent abrogates any necessity for economy, grammar, coherence, or architecture of speech. Mozart's Turkish music was a joke. What some of our contemporaries would do with a subject like *Il Seraglio* is only too easy to guess. There may indeed be yet in store for us a setting of ' *Kennst du das Land ?* ' that will incorporate such local colours as seem now to be essential to the treatment of so geographical a theme.

Not that music must never widen its horizon. So far as new turns of speech, whatever their origin, can be handled with a sense of proportion, enriching the fabric rather than tearing it, they are on every ground to be welcomed. Their incorporation is the main problem, and it is a problem of values. When they are used merely as a kind of aural geography, they are an artistic disease.

The infusion of local dialects is one phenomenon, the resuscitation of the mediaeval modes is another, and there are important relations between them. In both cases it is the ' not-C ' element which is first stressed. It is indeed probably an anachronism strictly to apply the term 'mode' to these scales as they affect us to-day. We cannot recapture the purity with which they were regarded by the musicians who developed them. To us they are perforce related to the classical key-system, and it is their divergence from this that appeals to the modern ear. Could we return to the modal period there is no reason to suppose that we should do other than follow the path that was then traced. That they might remain pure and distinct the modes had to be rigid. Within their prescribed limits they were vehicles of a remarkable intimacy of expression. It was this that destroyed them. The most harmonically flexible of them in the end supplanted the others, for composers began to prefer one set of internal relations, unique and therefore a commanding pivot around which the imagination could circle, to a group of mutually exclusive values, the proper conservation of which was a problem of great nicety. Once the classical system had become axiomatic, the discarded remnants of other modes could be brought into relation with it, and it is in this direction that some of our contemporaries are finding a new outlook.

Folk-music offers a similar field and is approached from the same angle. What appeals technically to the musician is the survival of old scales in these melodies. They embody a dialect which has escaped the levelling power of the classics. It is the flattened seventh, the minor third with a major sixth, the features which are not major-minor in fact, which give them character. We cannot hear these folk-songs in their purity, as their less sophisticated composers did, and they therefore have for us, like the modes, a charm of diversion and digression which is not necessarily intrinsic. Could we live ourselves into them we should have to disregard all values classically derived, and it is probably true of them as of the modes that their expressive power lies substantially in their rigidity. The lack of character complained of in the major-minor system is due to the fact that it has been made to cover so wide a field of expression. It no doubt had, originally, as much or as little spice as any other convention.

A few bars from W. G. Whittaker's part-song, ' *Oh, I ha'e seen the roses blaw* ', exhibits the quality of texture often associated with the study of folk-music :

Its atmosphere has, to our ears, a certain relation to that of mediaeval modal music, but this derivation must not be pushed far. The neo-modal music of to-day is projected on a background of modern resources ; resources, both technical and formal, which it freely incorporates. It tries to make the best of both worlds, and the mixture certainly offers possibilities. Transferred to a more elaborate medium, it provides the flavour often characteristic of diatonic modernity. Ex. 95 is from Howells's Quartet in A minor.

The atmosphere consciously sought by a texture founded on these neo-modal or folk-song values will be made clear by the following example from Vaughan Williams's Three Rondels, *Merciles Beauty* :

Compare this with a setting of the same poem by Arnold Bax, and the contrast of styles is illuminating.

It is clear at once that although Bax is harmonically daring, he is true to the classical tradition, whereas Vaughan Williams, in spite of apparently greater simplicity, is actually a disciple of revolt. Bax sets the poem in the musical idiom of his own day, as Schubert or Schumann would have done. Vaughan Williams is consciously archaic, and in this particular work is true to the fashion which, in treating a subject that has a definable period or place, tries to incorporate associations of a like nature in the accompanying music. This neo-modal texture, when it keeps near to the system from which it is derived, sounds like quotation. When it is chromatically flexible, as is often the case, it may not yet have found a stable equilibrium relative to the classical medium, but it points the way to an expansion of idiom based on values other than those of the major-minor system.

A modern mode which has already worn threadbare is the whole-tone scale. In very small doses it has a certain pleasant vagueness. In substantial quantity it is unbearably monotonous, and its fertility is of the scantiest. It is killed by its own logic. The equality of its melodic steps robs them of significant value. They are like the six sides of a regular hexagon, totally devoid of relative meaning. The available combinations of intervals are also soon exhausted, and whole-tone scales have but two 'keys', a semitone apart, exactly alike, yet with no note in common. Neither do they offer any chord that is unambiguously related to any other scale. These negations, and the added fact that whole-tones are phonetically 'soft', account for the rapid diminution of interest in any sustained texture of this kind. Debussy tried hard to make something out of it. Ex. 98 is in one of the whole-tone 'keys' (*Cloches à travers les feuilles*), Ex. 99 is in the other (*Préludes : Book I : 'Voiles'*).

8va .... *8va* ......

The latter is part of what appears to have been an attempt to write a whole movement in this scale. But Debussy himself could not bear it, and at the one climax of the prelude he abandons it for a more significant medium. It is the internal irregularities of a scale that give it expressive power.

Discussion of the whole-tone scale ought, however, to be qualified by the admission that although many composers, following Debussy, have used it as a system consonant in itself, few have experimented with its potential dissonances, if one may thus borrow and apply the old technical terms. Each of the two whole-tone scales has six notes within it, and six without. The latter are ' discords '. They are therefore available for providing the same kind of expressive variety which the traditional discords of the other systems offer. Scriabine seems to have had some such intuition in *Prometheus*. The first chord of this work, quoted in Ex. 35, is a complete whole-tone chord, and an inversion of the chord noted in Ex. 38, provided the F sharp in it is taken to be an appoggiatura between F natural and G. Later passages in *Prometheus* seem to leave no doubt that this is the grammar of the matter. We give two verbatim, adding a square bracket between each ' discordant ' note and its ' resolution '. All the other notes in the passages are contained in the chosen whole-tone chord.

Prometheus consists largely of these harmonic novelties. Scriabine also discovered how strange are the variations in implied tonality which inversions of such chords can give, though the actual notes concerned remain the same. He did no more, however, than follow his usual practice of reiterating a few chosen formulæ. Theoretically, he only touched the fringe of the subject.

There are two composers in particular, however, whose works may be said to represent the *ne plus ultra* of contemporary expansion through this radical broadening of the essential stuff of music. They are Bartòk and Schönberg. The listener confronted without preparation by mature examples of the styles they may be said to represent is conscious of little more than chaos, both melodic and harmonic. It seems impossible to relate such impressions to anything even remotely connected with previous experience, and one's first inclination is to say that either we or they are musically mad. Yet there is a clear gradation of texture in both, steep as it undoubtedly is, and whatever may be the ultimate value or influence of their achievement, it offers admirable illustrations of the tendency under discussion.

Bartòk is a Hungarian, and is so far in the fashion of our day that he does not disguise the fact. He does not subject his native prepossessions to the veneer of cosmopolitanism. Rather does he accentuate his own idiom, an idiom to which classical technique may, if it can, adhere, but which will admit of no emasculating

106

compromise. This, at least, is how we read his art. Europe already knows something of Hungarian folk-music. Its ears have been frequently tickled by queer tunes dressed up in pseudo-classical clothes. It is these foreign clothes that Bartòk will not have. The texture must be as original as the melodic line, must grow out of it, and it is therefore not surprising that to those who find his melodic material, whether original or derived, essentially foreign, his texture is at first incomprehensibly strange. Of the processes of Bartòk's mind something may be seen through examples selected to this end from one little group of pianoforte sketches. The reader will realise, however, that the more unfamiliar a style, the more necessary it is that it should be known in substantial quantity. We cannot do more than give isolated passages that have many parallels in what we conceive to be Bartòk's technical evolution.

(101)

Here we have a scale of marked individuality and of five notes only. The whole melody of which this is a fragment never moves outside these limits. It has formal coherence of the clearest kind. Phrases are repeated and varied with orthodox artistry. It is a melody of the early folk-song type, and in order to make clear what is the foreign element in it, let us indulge in the schoolboy game of paraphrasing it in other and more familiar pentatonic scales. Substitute for D sharp either D natural or C sharp, and all the internal values of the tune become normal to our ears.

(102) a   b

Bartòk's melodic divergence is radical, and the accompaniment is equally distinctive, providing no more than an occasional background for the melodic flavour. In Ex. 103 this function is clearer still. The bass hardly pretends to harmonise, in the classical sense, and it is difficult not to regard it as suggesting a new kind of value, more elaborate and more flexible than the drone of primitive music, but as yet without the formal distinction of harmony as such. The extreme economy of statement which is often a feature of Bartòk's work is also well shown.

The melody is itself remarkable. It touches during its whole course nearly every note in the chromatic scale, and yet there is of course no single interval in it which, did it occur in a melody of traditional character, would sound unfamiliar. It is this absence of the normal context which robs Bartòk's detail of its associations, and though we may, intellectually, admit his melody to be coherent, it is for us imaginatively thin. It has no sure place in our melodic consciousness, and to this extent it lacks meaning and warmth. What may happen when two such themes are combined is shown in the following examples :

The first phrase of Ex. 104 is very deceptive, because the hearer cannot help relating it to diatonic memories, the more so because Bartòk first enunciates it in still simpler terms than are here quoted. ' Here is a tune at last'. But this attitude is mistaken. It is the whole section given which is really Bartòk's sentence, and if this sentence is coherent in expression, then the initial notes have a purport quite other than that which classical precedents would lead one to expect. Chromaticism in extreme degree must include all the scales we know, and the law of averages alone would guarantee occasional sensations of reminiscence. That may indeed be the end of the journey ; a fringe of the old diatonic consciousness occasionally invading a music of pure chromaticism.

The last bar of Ex. 104 provides a new and distinctly expressive phrase, which is then immediately combined with the first phrase, as in Ex. 105. The curious reader should play this passage until it is reasonably familiar. It has almost a hypnotic effect. One is gradually but inexorably drawn towards a goal which is outside previous experience. Considered formally, the passage is undeniably coherent, yet the more concentrated it becomes the more vague or fantastic is its meaning. This is true of Bartòk and Schönberg alike. When their texture is complex it ceases to grip the mind. It is, traditionally, incomprehensible, and the impressions

109

it leaves are either æsthetically vague, as of indeterminate inflection or cadence, or chiefly dynamic, as of more or less movement, accent, reinforcement, and the like. It is when they play, as they often do, with simple strands of thought, that the flavour of other-worldliness is most pronounced. And whether this other world be a better or a worse, it is at least a proof that the impulse that creates it is the fruit not so much of evolution, classically considered, as of revolution, and of a revolution that involves fundamental reassessments of the values hitherto current.

In Schönberg the stimulus of a local dialect is not apparent. We seem rather to be at grips with a process of intellectualisation which has finally divorced expression from all traditional roots. Schönberg was at first noticeably orthodox, in the post-Wagnerian manner. Then in a very short time he developed for himself a texture the consistent strangeness of which has no contemporary parallel in the work of any composer so initially gifted. Yet there are stages in this development which are not without prophetic implications. The String Quartet, Op. 10 furnishes examples.

(106)

This quotation is the cadence of the first movement. The sustained chord embroidered by the unusual chromaticisms of the viola is a combination that undoubtedly grows expressive to the point of complete assimilation—on the one condition, however, that it shall, as it does, ultimately resolve into the tonality which it may figuratively be said to be seeking: that of the movement, F sharp minor.

(107)

Ex. 107 is the end of the second movement. It is technically allied to Ex. 106. In both movements the key-
feeling is always highly attenuated, and for considerable periods is completely obscured by virtue of complex
and conflicting chromaticisms that cannot be associated
with even the most recondite classicism. The second
movement is in D minor, so far as one may hazard a
generalisation of relations so tenuous. It ends as quoted,
the statement of key being reduced to a single note,
D, and this after long preparatory passages of the most
atonal type. See also Ex. 108 below, where the passage
ending at the pause ' resolves ' into a suggestion of D
minor, wholly contained in the two quiet notes which
follow.

(108)

Can the sense of a classical resolution be possibly
economised further ? Compare the ten or a dozen
final common chords that used to be considered essential to the establishment of a tonality that had never
been left more than a thought's-length away. Compare
the end of the first act of *Pelléas et Mélisande* (Ex. 45),
where Debussy carefully resolves his ending more than
once before leaving it suspended with hardly more
than the last full-stop of the sentence omitted. What
will happen if Schönberg does the same ? What is left
when the last bars of the above examples are omitted ?

III

What is then left is the texture of the later Schönberg, of which the following are examples taken from
his piano pieces* :

(109)

(110)

These passages do not actually occur at the end of their
respective movements, but they differ in no essential
respect from progressions that do represent finality
in this sense. They are chosen for quotation because
they are simple, restrained, coherent, even expressive
in a vague way. They have everything indeed but
meaning, as we have tried to define it. There is no
interval or chord in them that cannot be found in
works of classical derivation, but the definite orienta-
tion of an intelligible context which alone can give a
system expressive values is to all appearances completely
absent. There is no help for it. Significance is not
absolute, but relative. 'When everybody's somebody,
then no one's anybody'. If and when chromaticism
has destroyed the conventional scales which give it
meaning, then it will either have to adopt new conventions or else die of aimlessness.

Schönberg retains the formal devices which are

* In transcribing these examples, I have not spared the reader the
generous measure of unnecessary accidentals with which Schönberg
has seen fit to encumber his scores. His work is difficult enough to
read, in all conscience. As he often writes it, it is simply maddening.

traditional : repetition, variation, imitation, development, and so forth. The following passage from the *Five Orchestral Pieces* (Op. 16) will show how frankly academic he can be in this respect, so far as mere outline goes. What is lacking throughout these later works is the whole category, root and branch, of melodic and harmonic values as they have hitherto been understood. and this omission is obviously deliberate and fundamental.

(m)

One is tempted to ask what, if any, is the meaning of this music, in the artistic sense, to Schönberg himself, or to his imitators and admirers. Diffidently, for it is greatly daring to venture on the diagnosis of a mentality so endowed as Schönberg's earlier works have proved his to be, we may perhaps be allowed to suggest, of two things, one. It is conceivable that to Schönberg himself the classical values are still there. The extreme and growing attenuation of them, which to the hearer seems finally to have snapped the bond completely, may still be present to the composer, giving his ideas a significance to him which the hearer is unable to grasp. These variations in sensitiveness are universal. To the uncultivated ear Bach may be hardly more comprehensible than Schönberg. What is extreme in Schönberg's case is that unprejudiced study brings so little understanding to the mind. Then the critical failures of our predecessors begin to haunt us, and we are apt to conclude that lack of imaginative endowment is always the prerogative of the critic, never of the composer. This is a great assumption. May not the composer himself be writing in an unknown tongue, or in a shorthand peculiar to himself? May it not be a failure on his part that prevents that reciprocal relation which is comprehension? Posterity may succeed in deciphering his script, but this also is pure assumption. There is a degree beyond which the esoteric becomes inhuman.

Alternatively, and this, though tentative, is an explanation that would seem to agree with many of the facts, Schönberg may have intellectualised the phenomena of increasing historical expansion into a system which amounts logically to pure chromaticism. In this medium he writes, and the product has no positive relations, nor is it designed to have any, with the traditional values of his forerunners. If this be true, however, he is hardly in better case. His contribution to music then becomes akin to that of the primitive man who first cut a few random holes in a reed and extemporised on the sounds so produced. He may have fashioned the material medium of an art, but he is not yet an artist. Not until his sounds are organised into a communicable system of relations, associations, values, will the product be what is understood by the art of music. If Schönberg and his followers are extemporising in this way, with the sole difference, and it is only a difference of degree, that their medium is the whole elaborate apparatus of music as it exists to-day, then they are exploiting what may conceivably become the vehicle of a certain degree of expression, but they cannot hope to find any but the very vaguest communicable values in it. Intellectual craftsmanship there may be, but not true imaginative significance, for the imagination has not, in such a primitive medium, the recognisable landmarks that might give its flight

114

direction and purpose. When men are addressed in a language foreign to them, the sounds may be articulate, the tone of voice persuasive, impassioned, vehement, and so forth, but that is all the meaning they can extract. If it be a language of the speaker's own invention, then he is, and will for long if not for ever remain, to all intents and purposes dumb.

This discussion of texture is at an end. It has at least two serious flaws. It has concentrated attention on technical daring, and has therefore presented a picture of contemporary music from one angle only, and that not necessarily the most important. There have been not a few great artists who invented little but consolidated much. Further, and for this the variety of its subject matter may be held responsible, it has pursued a scheme of classification which may find a certain justification so far as it assists the analytical inquirer, but which should not be taken as more than a convenient form of presentation. Three tendencies have been outlined, the further evolution of classical harmony, the multiplication of tonalities, and the search for a more complete chromaticism. How shadowy are the boundaries between these divisions will be seen in a final example from Stravinsky, whose technique was in the main identified, and in many respects legitimately identified, with the phenomena of multiple tonality.

Ex. 112 is from the *Chant du Rossignol*. How many of the remarks applied to Bartòk, for instance, could not also be applied to the first four bars of the following passage ? The melody is perhaps just a little nearer to tradition, near enough it may be to express a rarefied yet unmistakable beauty. The arpeggios again are akin to Bartòk, with perhaps just a little more flavour of an old form, if not of the old substance. And the chords that are afterwards wrapped round these two ideas are very near Schönberg, though again their is more sequence, if not more intrinsic consonance. It is at

these fringes of resemblance that classification is a clumsy device. No juggling with formulæ will serve. Discrimination must be as vital and as subtle as music itself, for in the harmonic consciousness, as elsewhere, all extremes meet.

THE PROBLEM OF ARCHITECTURE

‘ A thousand originalities are produced by defect of
faculty, for one that is produced by genius. For in the
pursuit of beauty, as in that of truth, an infinite number of paths lead to failure, and only one to success ’.
George Santayana : ‘ The Sense of Beauty ’.

HITHERTO we have been considering what
may be called the sound-stuff of contemporary
music. Various matters of more general application have been discussed incidentally, but it has been
usually possible to illustrate these with reference to
details of technique which could either be quoted or
defined. No view of our subject would, however, be
even partially complete which did not embrace at least
a consciousness that greater than the invention of new
expedients is the handling of them, and that in the
problems of extended form there is required a power
of balance and synthesis which is just as real as it is
difficult to describe. No art can subsist on details,
however prolific or ingenious these may be. Many of
the devices that have been noted are as yet hardly more
than tentative explorations. No one composer, no group
of composers. can claim to have mastered them all.
But even were this power never so widely granted, it
would not in itself be any guarantee of the ultimate
artistic stature of our time. Many of the supremely
important movements in artistic history have been
severely restricted both in time and place, and have
been bounded by formal conventions of uncompromising rigidity. The arts of Greece, the renaissance in
Italy, the culture of Elizabethan England, to name a
few outstanding examples, were phenomena as remarkable in their æsthetic restraints as in the universality

of the forms of expression based on these foundations. And it has therefore seemed to many of the most thoughtful critics that if we would emulate past achievements we must be prepared to concentrate our thought on particular rather than on general forms of sensitiveness. It is some such instinct which many artistic associations and cliques have behind them, for it is an undoubted truth that great works of art come not by wealth of resource, but by intensity of imagination. Where we so often differ from the local or temporal associations of the past lies in our seeking a conscious and artificial boundary, a segregation which is intellectual rather than æsthetic. Greece, Italy, and England embraced, as they thought, the whole known world of experience. Their conventions came from within, from a process of selection which marked and cemented the artistic views of the artist and his friends alike. It was not fear of distraction which influenced them, but an unerring instinct of choice. Thus were they able to concentrate in one or in a few artistic forms an experience which acknowledged no limits. This appears to be one of the many distinctions between their day and ours. They selected imaginatively, intuitively, almost unconsciously, relating every detail to some accepted standard of æsthetic worth. We, intent on new devices, are in danger of missing this broader conception of value, and it is doubtful whether any merely intellectual grasp of the difficulty can adequately help us.

Granted so much, we may proceed to discuss the problem of formal architecture in music from a point of view akin to that already adopted in earlier chapters. Analysis of these matters is always somewhat artificial, but there is a sense in which the creation of a work of art may be represented as a conflict between the energy of inspiration and the inertia of form. The fight is sometimes so severe that the product shows obvious scars. Michelangelo compelling his imagination to

118

think in terms of a particular block of marble is a phenomenon which has parallels in every sphere of artistic endeavour. The imagination may demand what the technical material cannot supply. These are often the failures of the potentially great. Poverty of talent, on the other hand, may attempt to dress itself in clothes that are too big for it. The failures of lesser men are frequently of this kind. And success may be similarly analysed.

It sometimes happens that an artist is prepared to devote the whole of his intellectual energy to the fashioning of a technical instrument adequate to the expression of the most subtle or original intuitions. This was essentially the method of Bach and of Wagner, widely though they differed in the demands they made. Bach spent more time in the pursuit and practice of technical ideals than any composer before or since. His method was, as we have already had occasion to note, the development of a melodic texture to a degree capable of practically unlimited wealth and variety. Wagner too, from another angle, forged his own tools. These were both processes of more or less conscious evolution. They involved a sustained effort towards technical perfection, and their success was in both cases phenomenal. Great intellectual were combined with great imaginative gifts, and the two kept pace. The imagination never wavered, and the intellect enlarged its sphere unceasingly. Such patience and such application are not only rare in themselves, but still more rarely are they allied to creative endowments such as both Bach and Wagner commanded.

Equally rare is the composer of high rank whose intuitions are of such a nature that no kind of formal rigidity appears to disconcert him. Mozart is, in music, a supreme, if not indeed a unique, example of this complete and effortless accord between inspiration and form. He could and did accept, apparently without a suspicion of discomfort, the conventional formulæ which he found to hand, and he invested everything he touched with an atmosphere of freedom and resiliency that has been, and is likely for long to be, without parallel. His imagination appears to play unrestrained within the narrowest limits. He is never mechanical, yet every creative impulse seems but to render still more perfect the balance of his formal models. Fashions of design were to him not obstacles but opportunities. They became in his hands the most innocent and engaging companions. That there should be anything in the nature of a technical problem seems hardly to have entered his head. He assimilated in infancy certain well-defined forms. Thenceforth whatever he had to say, lyric or dramatic, grave or gay, sacred or secular, seemed to fit into a few precise patterns as a hand fits into a glove. Something has already been said of the factor of range in expression Mozart did not as a rule attempt those long flights which have often challenged and defeated men of very great gifts. But it is none the less a source of perennial wonder to the student to see how Mozart, in what may be imaginatively a most fluid or dramatic situation, will suggest characters, illustrate moods, accompany any and every variety of action, and at the same time preserve not only an extreme purity of melodic or harmonic diction, but with it an undisguised technical formality which is as precise and regular as it is unfailingly alive.

It is beside these two ideals of formal perfection, of Bach and Mozart respectively, that we would for a moment place the more explosive force of Beethoven. He too, though his personality was too fiery to fit into any mould, either of his own or of another's making, grappled tirelessly with the problems of form. Beethoven did not so convincingly achieve that formal poise which in many respects distinguishes Bach above all composers of comparable rank, but his scars were those of a giant. Beethoven stretched his forms, as he stretched himself, almost to breaking point. And if, to give one example, he failed at the end of the Choral Symphony to surpass himself in the expression of that extreme exaltation towards which he was clearly striving, it must be allowed that never before had a composer set himself the task of excelling the heights which Beethoven had, in the march of that symphony, already scaled. The personality of Beethoven has overshadowed a century of European music, just as the personality of his contemporary, Napoleon, has overshadowed a century of European politics. He produced some of the greatest works, as he no less certainly produced some of the most dangerous models, that music has to show. He left thirty-two piano sonatas and nine symphonies, yet the more intimately they are known the less can one hazard even a guess as to what the thirty-third sonata or the tenth symphony would be like. They would be Beethoven, and that is but the statement of a formal enigma. How many movements they would have, and which would be which ; what would be the psychological mood of any or all of them, either in detail or as a whole ; whether the themes would be slight and the handling sublime; whether there would be an orgy of rhythm or a feast of melody, or both ; whether they would follow an old form or invent a new one ; all these are matters on which nothing intelligible can be said. He would state, in some new and surprising way, ideas which so soon as they were grasped would seem to be as inevitable as they were unaccountable. We talk somewhat glibly of sonata-form and attach it to the name of Beethoven. There never was a greater deception. It is no doubt possible to extract from his movements two themes and a coda, and to say that here is, or might be, or should be, a double bar, and so forth. But it is often equally possible to extract three or four or five themes, though what will be their order or importance is beyond anyone to lay down. The first movement of the *Eroica*, a comparatively early work, has two supremely important sections, one of which first occurs after the conventional exposition is at an end, and the other after the whole movement, by every traditional principle of design, should have reached its full-stop. The late sonatas and quartets are admitted to be beyond formal classification. But the true Beethoven was always beyond classification. He was descended in a measure from Haydn and Mozart, but it is none the less true that the moment we recognise his models we lose him. The things he himself said were just those that had no place in his inherited architecture. Beethoven is the creative iconoclast. A new Beethoven, should he come, will defeat our legislation, be it never so broad. He will be clumsy, he will be vehement, yet there will be a tenderness as well as a warmth of passion in him, and to this might be added an Olympian sense of humour, an attribute which our veneration always tends to hide. What in others would be incoherence, might in him be very near to ultimate truth. Criticism must approach Beethoven with care. His was a divine madness.

But if Bach and Mozart may be taken as the twin poles of formal perfection, and Beethoven as the explosive genius that cannot be confined, then the main critical task of our day is to answer the following question. Are there any standards of judgement that will cover the work of these great exemplars, standards that can also be applied with fair consistency to the music of any period and of any place ? No narrow technical values will serve, because as between Bach and Mozart there is no identity of technical aim. Nor is it possible to point to any particular form as the key. If those qualities that convince us of the supremacy of their work can be defined at all, they must indicate values that are above and beyond the particular dress in which these men respectively clothed them. Analyses of this kind will naturally tend to overlap, but it would seem that there are at least two factors, two angles of approach, as it were, to the appreciation of intrinsic artistic worth, to which even Beethoven might intellectually subscribe, while Bach and Mozart, notwithstanding extreme differences of outlook, would support them without reservation. And these two qualities can also be applied to the art of any time or place. One of them we shall venture to call the factor of economy, the other that of coherence. These particular terms are approximations; they are not in any sense technical definitions. They cannot be exclusively described by any one or by any ten examples, and they will often overlap. But they do represent sufficiently definite reactions to experience to be capable of a broad application to values of all kinds.

By economy is meant the fitting use of material. It is not necessarily a demand for simplicity. There is the Mozart of the *Requiem* as well as the Mozart of the Sonatas, just as there is the Bach of the *B minor Mass* and the Bach of the French Suites. A trivial idea grandiosely set out ; a greater idea marred by technical whims ; these are failures of economy in this sense. And on a more material plane the same standard holds good. Confusion between a technique of the piano and a technique of the orchestra, between what is vocal and what is instrumental ; faults of this kind have already been discussed. Simpler still, there is the pianist who does not listen to his own playing, whose intentions are never tested by their actual results. All these are failures of economy. They are a waste or a misapplication of means.

Coherence is to be understood as coherence of style. It is that which relates the detail of a work to the whole of it ; which does not permit incongruous aberrations of fancy. An idea that is striking, or ingenious, or whimsical, be it never so ably expressed, is not everywhere in place. There is involved in all artistic work of high rank the paramount importance of choice. A composer who does not sift his ideas with reference to something in the nature of an inclusive vision, whether

123

it be conscious or intuitive, is either careless or undiscriminating. Should a stanza of Swinburne suddenly occur in a poem by Burns, that would be the kind of incongruity which is æsthetically incoherent. Isolated verses may each be good of their kind, but if they have no common standard of fitness they will never coalesce into a poem. Coherence involves, as it were, a reference of details to the same plane of experience. It is not a question of being exclusively either grave or gay. It is a sense of balance, of fitness, of æsthetic level. We feel it throughout in works of tried repute. Their style never caricatures itself, so to speak. It is never irrelevant, or distracted, or aimless, having regard to the prevailing atmosphere of thought. Some such prevailing temper is essential.

These two forms of artistic discipline, economy of statement and coherence of style, do not of course affect what has already been said as to the intelligibility of a composer's primary intuitions. The later Schönberg, for example, might frequently emerge with a certain credit from an examination which ignored the necessity for intrinsic meaning in the actual stuff of thought. We propose now to take for granted a composer's credentials in this respect. Let the actual material of his thought be at least within reach of experience, his originality an expansion or a synthesis of tradition. There remains his attitude towards the material he uses, and his power to sustain a consistent fertility of imagination. These qualities will profoundly affect his grasp of architectural form.

Of the internal economies of music much has already been noted in the discussions of melody, rhythm, and texture. In some directions the twentieth century has made noticeable advances. Never were the individual characters of instruments and their balance in combination so well understood. It was rare, fifty years ago, to find a composer who could handle the orchestra along any but traditional lines. Now it is rare to find

124

even a young aspirant who does not show a genuine power to gauge imaginatively internal delicacies of colour. Clumsy orchestration is almost a thing of the past. Similarly, we have all learnt to listen to the piano in a way that only the ablest of our forefathers could equal. Compare the technical address of Liszt in this respect with the far more pianistic attitude of Debussy. Liszt is seen at once to be frequently rather a transcriber for the piano than a thinker in its peculiar values. Debussy, Ravel, Scriabine, and many others have really mastered the piano ; its vertical bias, its melodic thinness, its arpeggios, its aptitude for blurred effects and hence for the suggestion of colour rather than line ; all these attributes are now common knowledge. And the same is true of instruments generally. Apart from the musical quality of what is given them to do, which is another and quite separate problem, they are handled with consistent skill, and players have responded loyally to the demands of enhanced and specialised technique. The voice alone is often an unrescued Cinderella, set to the most menial tasks, and in danger of forgetting her royal birthright. It was Wagner who appeared to encourage the modern fashion of what may be called words without song. He had a certain dramatic justification. But his successors have spread the practice into all kinds of vocal music, pure or otherwise, and some of our contemporary attempts to write song without words are often not so much a return to the melodic values of the past, as the substitution, for what at its best was the twin art of poetry and song, of an intellectual abstraction which is neither.

But the power to use instrumental material has undoubtedly outstripped the power to think in terms of a music that would translate this wealth of means into an equal wealth of beauty. The stereotyping of material combinations is a feature of our time which is far more widely applied than is sometimes realised.

125

There is a kind of mass-production of music which is almost as ruthless as the mass-production of machines. If a composer can think orchestrally at all, it is too much taken for granted that he will think to the orchestral dimensions of three trombones and a tuba. It becomes very difficult to find a public niche for ideas that will not tolerate so rigid or so quantitative a view. It was not considered improper, a century ago, to mix chamber and orchestral works in the same programme. There may, of course, be much to be said for designing concerts with reference to a certain technical unity. But our present fashion is at least as much administrative as æsthetic. We have developed a kind of avarice with respect to the keeping of nine-tenths of our orchestra silent while the other tenth might play the Schubert Octet. The net result is that the Octet rarely appears at all; while the contemporary composer who may have the temerity to think in combinations accounted unconventional may find, unless he enjoys some other means of advertisement, that his work comes into the world stillborn. And as a corollary to this it follows that our orchestral programmes contain a noticeable proportion of works, both old and new, which are only orchestral by convention. They are not the fruit of ideas that could only be properly expressed in so elaborate a medium. Fortunately there are signs of a reaction in favour of the chamber orchestra, though no such organisation is as yet safely launched. The size of the modern full orchestra is rapidly reaching a stage which it is impossible financially to maintain. What æsthetic discernment has as yet been unable to bring about may be achieved by a less fitful agent. Will the day ever come when mere size will have nothing to do with music ? Will musicians ever again be satisfied with just so many parts as they can think in, and no more ? Shall we ever return even to the comparatively fluid scores of the Brandenburg Concertos ? There are indications. Composers are turning to chamber music, not alone for the combinations which have traditional prestige, but for various small groups of instruments which seem apt for the effects desired. And there is perhaps a little less of the piano in this context, a circumstance of decided promise. The piano can too easily be made to cover a multitude of contrapuntal sins.

It is just possible that we are feeling our way towards that ideal combination, a small orchestra of soloists, in which every performer will be an aristocrat, to his own and to music's great advantage. Nobody knows yet what to do, still less what may eventually be done, with such a medium. There are few composers who can handle as many as a dozen instruments with sustained yet ordered independence. But no one ever did know what to do with new possibilities. Slowly, clumsily, and with but a partial dawning of comprehension, music has gradually embraced its resources. In the end one can imagine the new Bach, as it were, consummately applying the interpretative gifts of a selected few to the evolution of new forms of beauty. There was never a time when players of such perfection awaited the composer of genius. The old Bach was sometimes constrained to enrol an instrumental chorus to support his scanty soloists. We have seen where that may lead, and the new Bach will, it is to be hoped, be spared such temptations. This new music will in many respects be eclectic. It will not lend itself to arrangement for the piano, or submit to the devastating effect of unsuitable instruments in undiscriminating hands. But the vast concourse of music-lovers wants to listen, not to play. And now that difficulties of reproduction and circulation are for the most part solved, it is theoretically possible for new works to reach, in substantial purity, the ear of the true amateur, whoever or wherever he may be. The means are with us. What is needed is the hand to fashion and the will to advance them. There is always room for a great master.

What will certainly not serve any artistic end is the translation to small combinations of the mannerisms that may be tolerable or fashionable on a larger canvas. The string quartet which is orchestral is a poor string quartet. It is not that talented men have any difficulty in adapting ideas and making them effective by treating one violin as if it were twelve, and four instruments as though they were played by one keyboard This can be done, and done convincingly. But every success of this kind destroys the values proper to a quartet and, what is still worse, vitiates the taste of those who are led to approve it. This latter is the real misfortune. That one man should abandon himself to the more ingenious tricks of his trade is not of much account to the discriminating. But should his success prevent the more scrupulous from obtaining even a hearing, then the damage may, for its time and place, be irreparable. Tricks of the trade are what contemporary music chiefly suffers from. Because it is now possible to build up facile effects, it is difficult to keep clear of them. There are to be found, for example, in the contemporary repertory of the pianist scores if not hundreds of pieces, many of them under the signatures of gifted men, which are nothing but the twentieth-century version of Thalberg's *Home, Sweet Home*. This is indeed perhaps a little hard on Thalberg, because beneath his trimmings there was at least something of a tune. What is curious is that many of these contemporary pieces would scorn a frankly popular appeal. They frequently embody harmonic or rhythmic devices of very advanced types, and they are occasionally accepted as authentic by confessed missionaries of the new faith. It would be tedious to multiply instances. They exist in every department of contemporary effort. Perhaps one characteristic example of this juggling with novelty will serve.

The technical address of Stravinsky is beyond all question. There is nothing in the actual handling of

128

musical apparatus that presents the slightest uncertainty to him. His originality and his ingenuity are alike phenomenal, and he has had a marked effect on the technique of his time. There is also much in his work which is, by any unprejudiced standard, both new and beautiful. For the moment let us forget such aberrations as the Chinese March in *Le Rossignol.* Similar grotesques find a place in many of his works, and for them he can advance the excuse of the theatre. It seems now to be an accepted maxim that if there is oddity on the stage there must be horse-play in the orchestra. It is in pure music that the issue is clearer. There may be in the literal *Histoire du Soldat* a vulgarity equal to that of the music. But there are the little piano pieces, which not even Stravinsky's most ardent disciples can defend without a twinge. There are the *Three Pieces for String Quartet.* One quotation from these latter has already been given (Ex. 86). Here is another :

Now if this type of passage has any proper place in the art of the string quartet, then the end is near. It is not here a question of a new idiom, or of an unfamiliar arrangement or concentration of ideas. There are no ideas, musically speaking. It is neither melody, nor rhythm, nor part-writing, nor harmony. It is just so much noise. The notes are recognisable, but then notation alone ensures so much. It is perhaps not altogether an unmixed tragedy that our notation has its limits. And the players are not yet invited to play on the other side of the bridge. This privilege may still await them, however, for Stravinsky does already go so far, in this particular movement, as to ask the second violin and viola, with a view to a special effect, to hold their instruments the other way up, 'like a violoncello'. As it stands, this example, which is not noticeably out of character in its setting, consists of the orchestral tricks of the *Chinese March*, arranged for a string quartet, with the tune left out.

The real conundrum is what Stravinsky himself thinks of these foibles. That he is serious is to be presumed, because his associates pay him the flattery of an imitation which is at least sincere to that extent. But if this be so, then there is no escape from the suspicion that Stravinsky is, to put it mildly, not over-scrupulous in the use of his material means. Or is his sensitiveness inherently patchy and intermittent ? Is *Pétrouchka* a lucky accident, as it were, a pantomime that happens to suit his irresponsible high spirits ? The wildest hammering must occasionally hit the nail on the head. Are Stravinsky's beautiful and convincing moments only the occasional successes of an unbridled fancy ? The alternative that he is sometimes deliberately hoodwinking his public is just as unsatisfactory, and more difficult to believe. There appears to be only one other possible explanation, and we must leave the reader to make his own choice. ' Sir ', said Dr. Johnson, ' a man might write such stuff for ever if he would abandon his mind to it '.

Economy of statement, then, is at least a fair criterion of an artist's attitude of mind. It is not so much a calculated less or more, as a certain intuitive weighing of words. Yet economy of the most devoted kind is not enough. There is something in the sweep of ideas which is greater than the effective statement of any or all of them. There is a sense of architecture which gives every detail an atmosphere of spontaneous coherence. Rarely, in works that have stood the test of time, do we feel that the composer has lost this perspective of the whole. Bach could have rewritten any of his movements in a dozen different ways. It is not one idea or one succession of ideas that is alone fitting. What is required is an æsthetic discernment which is constant in character throughout. A listener's consciousness that has become attuned and expectant by the exposition of what it presumes will be the prevailing emotional or imaginative colour of a work must not be suddenly or repeatedly distracted by ideas that are foreign to the chosen mood. It is this kind of unexpected shock which discomforts us when we find the tune *Land of Hope and Glory* in a march under the name of Elgar. Such a melody no doubt has, among its companions in the popular esteem, a certain value. What disconcerts us is the invasion, so to speak, of a melody of this type into the more sensitive work that we have learnt to consider characteristic of Elgar's maturity. We cannot conceive of such a lapse in connexion with the *Enigma* variations, for instance. These things do not happen in works of coherent worth. No incongruity of this kind occurs in the two great detached marches of Wagner.

Considered analytically, Bach approached the technical problem of coherence in two main ways. The simplest of these involved a consistent scheme of decoration. The first of the Forty-Eight Preludes is a perfect example of this device on a small scale. A succession of harmonies is rendered decoratively by a chosen form of arpeggio. Chopin's first prelude is an exact parallel to Bach's. There is an arch of plain masonry, so to speak, beautified by regular tracery. It is the arch which is really of primary importance, as many composers have found who thought decoration alone would serve. There must be a peak, as it were, in the harmonies, a design in the work as a whole, a solid and substantial symmetry, or the ornamentation is a waste of effort. Decoration can neither correct nor conceal an underlying failure of proportion. Multiply

131

a musical arch of this kind, varying the tracery, and
we have the form of variations, a form which has at
some time or other appealed to almost every composer
of the first rank. Schumann's *Etudes Symphoniques* are
like the successive bays which compose the nave of
a cathedral. Mozart's variations are the more homely
cloister. The principle of them all is the same, from
Byrd to Richard Strauss.

Bach's other method, and it was that in which his
most characteristic ideas were developed, was counterpoint. Something has already been said of this practice
as a foundation of texture. As architecture it is equally
significant. To Bach himself, and on his most extensive
plane, architectural coherence was almost literally the
art of fugue. It was the art, that is, of building up a
movement on one or more melodies of concentrated
import, which by their recurrence would hold the
fabric together, while their contrapuntal adventures
would give it life. It was essentially a guarantee of
imaginative unity. A texture of so homogeneous a
type might in the hands of mediocrity become dull,
but it could never encourage confusion of styles, while
to the composer gifted with both inventive genius and
a sense of proportion it was ideal, equal to any demands
either of expansion or elaboration that could be made
on it. Not that Bach usually wrote fugues from the
text-book angle. Text-book fugue is an abstraction,
like text-book harmony and counterpoint. It is music
minus imagination. But Bach's characteristic line of
approach to the architectural problem was fugal
counterpoint, and we have yet to discover a better.

Bach's coherence is like that of *Paradise Lost*.
Mozart's is like that of the *Faerie Queene*. To Mozart
coherence came by a sustained delicacy of versification.
He took his polished beads of melody and made them
into a necklace of pearls. The formal strings which
bound them and the little connecting knots which
separated them were of quite minor importance. His
132

stanzas, if we may adopt another simile, were often symmetrically arranged, sometimes as Sonatas, sometimes as Rondos, sometimes as dances. In any context it was the sustained magic of the single ideas and the delicate internal balance of the verses that made the poem. Architectural cohesion becomes almost an automatic result of this process. If a composer can write such melodies, we shall not quarrel as to how many of them go to make a movement. Then came Beethoven, who did not so much solve the formal problem as overwhelm it by a personal ascendancy. Yet there has remained both in him and in us enough of the Mozartian tradition to make us count as unworthy of the symphonic forms, either of Mozart or of Beethoven, any composer who could not bring to them the gift of lyric song. And the criterion by which the world has judged these formal melodies has always been this : that they must sustain, with respect to the symphonic style, a level of æsthetic diction adequate to the high light which a work of large proportions must inevitably throw on them.

After Beethoven, Wagner. Wagner was at first close to the harmonic texture of Beethoven, and he was also sympathetic to many aspects of Beethoven's dynamic style. He had a profound sense of proportion, but his plans were complicated by the peculiar demands which his chosen form entailed. His works were to be of the dimensions of a whole opera, an opera conceived not as a collection of lyrics, but as having something approaching the unbroken coherence of Bach. Whatever incidental flexibilities the drama might require, there was to be no failure of musical continuity. His solution of this problem has close connexions with the technique of Bach. He not only became in later years more and more contrapuntal, but the theory of form associated with his name is really an adaptation of the idea of fugue. His use of salient themes is, in its incidence, like Bach's use of a fugue subject. The musical adventures of the themes weave the pattern of the work, while their identity cements it as a whole. Bach's was the contrapuntal, Wagner's the harmonic or symphonic fugue. So far there is a parallel between them. But there was also a divergence. Bach's consistency was thorough. It was as true in section as in bulk. Broad changes of atmosphere could be met by breaking a long work into separate movements. Detailed changes were rare. Wagner's wishes were much more complex than this. He had to follow the incidence of a drama that had its own unique form. He had therefore to provide a music that should somehow obey ideas that were theoretically external to it, while retaining a convincing character of its own. It was a formidable problem, and thematic music-drama appeared to solve it. But this solution only works under certain conditions, and the neglect of these conditions has been responsible for more subsequent incoherences of style than any other factor in the whole of our inheritance.

In the first place, Wagner's scheme demands that the themes themselves shall be phenomenal in concentrated and unique expression. It is easy to attack or to defend his theories. What nobody has since succeeded in doing is to write anything approaching his music. Very occasionally we meet a passage that has something of the Wagnerian finality, so far as a particular atmosphere is concerned. The following fragment from Vaughan-Williams' *London Symphony* has something akin to Wagner's distinction in this respect:

(114)

So has Holst's 'Neptune' theme (Ex. 87) and Stravinsky's fragment from the *Chant du Rossignol* (Ex. 112). But these flashes are now few. In Wagner they exist by the score. There are themes in Elgar, as there are in Richard Strauss, which have some of the Wagnerian tradition in them, but they are rarely rugged enough; they have not as a rule that overpowering individuality which alone will stand the wear and tear of the Wagnerian setting.

And in the second place, Wagner's theory is unnecessary apart from some kind of alien and external drama. It was to this end that he developed it. If a theme is to be handled with marked freedom of style, then two circumstances only can make its adventures coalesce. They must either justify themselves as pure music, which means that they must be subject to some prevailing tone in the whole work. Or else there must be some provision of intelligible signposts which will elucidate the distractions that may not be convincing on musical grounds alone. The former was the method of Bach, Mozart, and Beethoven, and of the classical tradition generally. The latter was a theory which for Wagner included the stage, and for Strauss the programme. The question really at issue is whether Wagner's solution was a solution at all, if translated into consistent practice. Can any art live in subjugation to ideas that are external to itself ? If history has any meaning there seems to be no doubt of the answer. If the *Pastoral* symphony will not hold together without an external programme, then it is no better and no worse than the thousand naive and forgotten sound-pictures which have been written by composers of every age, from John Munday's meteorological *Fantasia* to Steibelt's *Storm Rondo*. If we have to remind ourselves that Don Quixote is charging the sheep in order to make Strauss's sounds intelligible, then what we are listening to is not, for us, music. The battle in *Ein Heldenleben* is in this respect exactly in the same plight as that once popular drawing-room piece, *The Battle of Prague*. Either it is music, battle or no, or it is not. If it is not music in this exclusive sense, no cleverness can save it. New forms of apparatus may offer new effects of realism, but every generation finds its predecessors childish in this matter. ' *Mehr Empfindung als Malerei* ', wrote Beethoven. He understated the case. ' All feeling and no painting ' would be safer. This is the essence of the problem. The power of external impressions to stimulate the æsthetic imagination is almost a description of the artistic impulse itself. But if these sensations are not in the first place completely sublimated and then re-expressed exclusively in terms of the particular art concerned, there can be no permanent worth in the product.

And this brings us to the last of the conditions which actually governed Wagner's practice. This is not the place to discuss the detail of Wagner's combination of three or four arts in one; acting, poetry, staging, music, or whatever further subdivisions might help the analyst. It will be enough to say that to produce a dragon, to describe a dragon, to act the fear of a dragon, and at the same time to make a noise expressive of a dragon, is a form of tautology open to serious criticism. Though Wagner preached the fusion of many arts into one, what he frequently did was to multiply every impression by four. How far this was due to the grain of his own sensibility, how far to his estimate of the public imagination, may be left to the reader to decide. What has justified him, what constitutes his achievement, what the whole world unites in honouring, is neither a theory of unities nor a heroic attempt to apply them. The place of Wagner in the arts is that of the greatest musician since Beethoven. He was a musician before everything, theory or no theory, and whenever there was real competition between the arts that he proposed to practise on equal terms, it was music which invariably won. He wrote his own drama, and

136

therefore presumably gave himself the musical opportunities he desired, but he had actually no more scruple about keeping the action in suspense while he said his say in music than had the most inveterate Italian of them all. The music became continuous; the action certainly did not, unless the slow growth of an æsthetic atmosphere is allowed to constitute action in this sense. Indeed, where Mozart and Verdi were content to leave their characters standing while they stole the five minutes necessary for a neat lyric, Wagner planted his firmly in some fixed situation while he appropriated half an hour to write a symphony about it. Wagner paid as much homage to the architecture of pure music as any composer who ever lived. Complaint is sometimes made that we spoil Wagner by playing extracts in the concert-room, though it is significant that this criticism often rests on the ground that each act, or indeed each opera, is a symphonic whole. Yet we rarely quote his verse, or play his dramas, without the music. It is otherwise with operas like *Pelléas et Mélisande* and *Salome*. *Pelléas* is probably the most satisfactory opera ever written, so far as the artistic unity of the theatre is concerned. Maeterlinck leaves so much to the imagination that there is room for Debussy to add a musical twilight. This he does with a restrained beauty which truly supplements the stage without dwarfing it. Wilde's *Salome* is of such dramatic intensity that Strauss can only follow it breathlessly, throwing to the winds the considerations proper to pure music, often content to add the fury of sound to the fury of action. We do not extract the dramatic music of *Pelléas* and *Salome*, though we play them as plays. The fact is that as pure music they are not sufficiently clear or sufficiently homogeneous, as almost every page of the mature Wagner is. But they are, as operas, much nearer to Wagner's theories than were his own, with perhaps the single exception of *Die Meistersinger*. But *Die Meistersinger* is quite literally a music-drama ; a drama,

137

that is, on the subject of music. No wonder Wagner made it into one long poem, from every point of view. It was an incarnation of his own most fundamental reactions. Wagner was a musician as Shakespeare was a poet. The dramas of Shakespeare are conceivable without his poetry, but it is the poetry that we instinctively associate with his name. It is the poet Shakespeare whom we worship. So it is Wagner the musician who commands us, first and foremost.

Out of the polemic of Wagner therefore, rather than out of his music, was extracted the notion that labelled themes, allied to an external story, might give us a coherent form. Under Wagner's own interpretation of this alliance, which gave music the casting vote in everything, the idea was plausible. Even a Bach fugue can be represented as a drama in music in which the subjects and counter-subjects are protagonists. But Richard Strauss sought for something more literal than this. If his story was to be intelligible without a stage, then there had to be in the music itself an emotional panorama so vivid that the sensitive hearer could interpret it almost exactly, given a few programme notes. Strauss sometimes actually achieved this. With the help of his sub-titles, it is possible to construe *Also sprach Zarathustra* almost into a reading of the book itself. Strauss had an amazing sensitiveness in this respect. But he was playing with fire. In the pursuit of more and more literal associations his attitude towards his material underwent a gradual and dangerous change. Wagner had created, as it were, new and pregnant musical ideas, to which he attached in his drama an emotion, or an action, or an object. Strauss began to think first of the object, or the circumstance, or the person, and to it he wedded a phrase that might sometimes be inspired, but sometimes was no more than ingenious; it was a conscious borrowing of associations. The distinction is not easy to define, but it is unmistakable. Compare Wagner's themes with
138

those of Strauss. Still more, compare the musical with the ingenious Strauss. At the same time Strauss's orchestral skill was tempting him to realism, and yet more symptomatic was the licence he began to exercise in the treatment of the themes themselves. The reader will remember the beginning of the *Meistersinger* Overture in its 'master' dress and in the later 'apprentice' version. It was ingenuity of this kind which seems to have fascinated Strauss. Musically it has a certain relation to Bach's diminutions or augmentations of a fugue subject. It carries also all the old dangers of mechanical application, plus a good many new ones of its own. Wagner's themes were, within narrow limits, markedly rigid. Therein lay their force. Like Bach's fugue subjects, they helped to preserve, as has already been said, a consistent æsthetic level. When Wagner sought a marked change of atmosphere he usually created new material. Thus there are many distinct themes closely associated with Siegfried, each characteristic of some attitude, or action, or possession, and so forth, and each preserved consistently to that end. Here Strauss parted company with Wagner. He began to augment, to diminish, to sentimentalise, to dignify, to parody, to caricature, to play every kind of prank with his chosen ideas. It was a process quite different to Beethoven's quips and jokes, for instance. In Beethoven's whimsical movements the material itself is generally whimsical from the first, and Beethoven does no more than underline this, with engaging candour. Strauss limited himself in no such way. His was a gradual but constant leaning towards clever manipulation in every direction at once. And when he was most ingenious he was least inspired. In the earlier symphonic poems he obeyed, like Berlioz and Liszt before him, the normal outlines of symphonic architecture. His themes were broad generalisations of emotional states, and he used them broadly. As time went on, however, he seemed to give way to a sort of

139

fever of literalism, and one of the clearest signs of it is this restlessness in the handling of themes. The reader will remember Exs. 24 and 25. *Don Quixote* also is naturally full of whimsicalities. And here are three statements of one theme from *Salome*.

(115)

(116)

(117)

Given a convincing explanation, in this case to be derived from the stage, why such radical contortions of material should occur at all, they are undeniably clever, expressive, and to the point, especially when the slightness of the connecting idiom is taken into account. But they are poles asunder in atmosphere, and it would require phenomenal powers of synthesis, both in the composer and in the listener, to make such ingenuities coalesce into a homogeneous style. This unscrupulous treatment of ideas may easily become, and without a jealous selective judgement it does infallibly become, a medley of incongruous patches. Combined with the temptations of an elaborate technique, it fosters a lack of poise which is perhaps the worst enemy to which a fine talent can succumb. Opinions may differ as to what actually happened to

Strauss. He chose subjects that seemed to repay illustration. Was it these that warped him ? Or was there a kink, as it were, in his original gift ? Strauss cannot be ignored, for when all is done and said he remains one of the outstanding figures and one of the outstanding influences of our time. Some of his work is as remarkable as anything that has been written since Wagner. And it is often pure music too. None the less is it true that Strauss gradually lost his judgement. The melodic gift, often of delightfully lyrical flavour, which appears so frequently in his songs and which has never altogether left him, tended to be increasingly overwhelmed by a mass of complexities and ingenuities of doubtful or external value. One is inclined to wonder whether he ought not to have pursued *Hänsel and Gretel* rather than *Elektra*. He chose the grand manner, and it frequently fell into the grandiose. There is in him a distinct wavering of that æsthetic level of thought which we are here concerned to examine.

This very brief survey of our formal inheritance should serve in great measure to define the practical architectural problem of our own day. A movement may deny its past. It cannot abolish it. The dynamics of Beethoven, the theories of Wagner, and the ingenuities of Strauss are still thoroughly alive. Public taste still tends to encourage extravagant fancy, both in the invention of ideas and in the handling of them, and by a perverse irony it then demands some kind of external explanation of these whims. This desire for literary or literal clues has been carried to such lengths that even Schönberg's *Five Orchestral Pieces*, than which there has probably never been a work more forbidding to the commentator, were furnished with sub-titles invented *ad hoc*, we are told, and against the initial desire of the composer himself. It became practically impossible to present a symphony as such, unless the composer already had a great reputation. It seemed as though a new claimant must first approach the public as anything in the world rather than a pure musician. As was well said : 'When will somebody write a Music Symphony' ?

Into this atmosphere have been flung the technical expansions already discussed. They are, like all augmentations of means, available either for use or for abuse. They can be attached to programmes or they can be left to find their own justification. In any event they add substantially to the problems of extended form. We have an embarrassing choice of inherited models, and we have innumerable novelties of technique which must either be definitely abjured or properly assimilated. It is this assimilation which is preliminary to architectural coherence, and to our century belongs the task of making these new factors, so far as it may find them fertile, coalesce into an intelligible standard of thought.

The attitude of some of our contemporaries is not without promise. The programme-complex can be disposed of by adopting titles that are indicative, when they can be said to indicate anything at all, of states of mind rather than of adventures in experience. Commentators can be humoured, and meanwhile the composer can dismiss the matter and write music. It is moreover to be noted that some men are prepared to attack the new problems of style in short flights, and with small means. This came naturally to the French. They were never really in tune with Wagnerian grandeur, their own reactions being as a rule either frankly spectacular or delicately neat. The symphonic stature of César Franck is an almost isolated exception to this rule. When therefore Debussy invented a harmonic style of decided originality he was often content to develop it in works that were either small in themselves or which involved as it were a panorama of impressions rather than an architecture of form. He and Ravel were in this respect the true disciples of Couperin and Rameau, and by confining themselves

142

to small proportions they were soon able to fashion their new ideas into a consistent if restricted whole. The more sensitive pioneers of an art have usually been content to advance by degrees. A century ago the young composer wrote symphonies, bad symphonies as a rule, but involving formally no more than the intelligent imitation of acknowledged authority. To-day it is taking serious risks to offer the new wine in such large quantities. It is not only very difficult for the public to digest, but it is also very difficult for the composer to handle. There is obvious danger in Scriabine's method, which amounts to the ruthless pursuit of a fixed idea, a pursuit which in his peculiar psychology is sometimes hardly to be distinguished from consistent hysteria. And there is perhaps greater danger still in those other extreme phenomena of our time, extended works built up out of a medley of themes as incongruous as can well be conceived. It is possible to find in one and the same movement bits of plain-song or folk-tune, harmonies of the fiercest novelty, together with rhythms and colours of dynamic vehemence and strange complexity. It is not a case of mixing Bach and Mozart. It is a mixture of Palestrina and Tchaikovsky. Indeed it is sometimes hardly a mixture at all. Ideas of every known derivation or quality are set nakedly side by side. Far more hopeful are the less pretentious pieces which are content to concentrate attention on one or on a few comparatively homogeneous thoughts ; and though the diversity of such works adds one more to the reasons that make a general view of our present endeavours seem so con-fused and confusing, it is in them that the hope of a coherent school of thought substantially lies. They show in bulk that motley profusion which is found in early virginal music. There we find pavanes and galliards, dances grave and gay, formless preludes and fantasias, variations on folk-song and plain-song, polyphonic toccatas and canzonas, all existing together in the loosest confraternity. There too we find composers of high distinction amusing themselves with little originalities of technique, like children with a new toy. That is where we seem to be to-day. Our apparatus is more complex, our models more numerous, but these are only differences of degree. If the reader will take a bird's-eye view of all the contemporary examples we have had occasion to quote, he will get an impression of the architectural difficulty far more vivid than any literary description of it can hope to give.

It has been for the most part outside the purpose of this essay to attempt to estimate the position of contemporary composers considered individually. Views of this nature that may have been expressed incidentally have been intended to illustrate principles or tendencies of thought. In a concluding page, however, an exception may be allowed, an exception which seems particularly suitable for the application of some of the values we have tried to define. The position of Frederick Delius in contemporary opinion is a curious one. He is no longer young, his mature work has been published and has been heard in bulk, and he has without any doubt completely assimilated an original and an essentially modern technique, in terms of a consistent level of thought. He has gained an almost universal respect, even from those to whom his particular angle of vision is not altogether sympathetic. There are some who consider the body of his work as a whole to be not only masterly as a means of expression, but unfailingly beautiful in its results. A few there are who hail him as incomparably the greatest musician of our time, though this opinion is sometimes urged with an impatience which to some extent defeats itself. Yet it is impossible to deny that the general appreciation of Delius is far from secure. In England he had an able and devoted missionary in Sir Thomas Beecham, who gave his work that practical support which is worth more than any number of literary advertisements.-The movement thus admirably inaugurated has not held its ground. It is said that we are too stupid or too inept to understand Delius; that he is better appreciated abroad. This may be so, though if the number of performances of his works given on the continent be divided by the number of orchestras and choruses available, not to mention the number of opera-houses, England may not emerge from the comparison so incorrigible a sinner as might at first sight appear. We are certainly no worse than Paris, to say the least. No, the present reputation of Delius is a phenomenon not of our locality, but of our time. How far has he himself contributed to it ? He is not aggressively an innovator, yet he distinctly belongs to the modern school. He seems indeed to represent, among the many crudities and exuberances of experiment, that ideal mean which should appeal to a similar level of public appreciation. Where lies the fault ?

In the first place, Delius has written little or nothing for the piano, or for those small combinations of instruments which are a very potent factor in the contemporary dissemination of music. There are admirable piano arrangements of most of his works, but they have to be read or played with imagination. His peculiar values, his essentially orchestral economy, suffer greatly when divorced from their proper medium. He also makes formidable demands on the technique of performance, on the understanding, and on the æsthetic sensibility of listener and performer alike. If one is not alert enough to listen, Delius will not periodically surprise one into wakefulness. He has no facile tricks, no seductive emotionalism, no nervous intoxication to offer. Neither is he telling a raw tale, nor cracking jokes. He is not overcome with a sense of his own technical capacity. All is not grist to his mill. There are many things now fashionable which he does not, will not, say. Complaint is sometimes made that there is so little one can carry away, so to speak, from Delius. But how much can one carry away, in this sense, from an unfamiliar work by Bach ? Delius has a melodic gift, but it is usually rhapsodic. He has an amazing harmonic instinct, but it is diffused. He does not distil his thought into a single line, nor into a striking passage. Delius is concerned primarily with texture, just as Bach was. It is a sustained atmosphere that he seeks, and texture is his approach to it. His method is harmonic ; Bach's was contrapuntal. But however fundamental this divergence may be technically, and however much one may doubt whether, so long as we think and play our parts horizontally, the more disparate impressions of harmony can hope to rival the sustained perfection of melodic counterpoint, this does not alter the fact that texture as such has æsthetic values of its own which may be derived neither from those of the single line nor yet from the reflected light of powerful harmonic themes. We do not demand from Bach the values either of Mozart or of Wagner. Delius learnt his art away from the schools, away from the fashions of his day. His diction has in it a tinge of aloofness, even of vagueness, which to some temperaments is a real difficulty. But he has at least one quality which is perhaps above all others scarce in our time ; he has a deep, a quiet, and an intrinsic sense of beauty. Is it this that our generation has lost or is losing ? His idylls *On hearing the first cuckoo in Spring* and *Summer night on the river*, and a dozen other movements of tranquil yet enchanted fantasy, were not born of the tumult of to-day. Like the idyll of Siegfried, they must be tasted without passion, without impatience. Delius is not of the market-place. So homogeneous is he that it is sometimes hard to tell where folk-song ends and Delius begins. It is hard to tell where is melody and where harmony. His is often a rhapsodic art, but still more is it at times an art of pure contemplation. And an art of pure

146

contemplation is not easy to practise in this twentieth century of ours.

And thus we reach the final question, so often raised, whether or no all or any of our present developments can aspire to permanent worth. To this we believe there is no clear answer. The ultimate fate of an artist rests not on his endowments alone. His fortune depends at least in equal measure on the æsthetic discernment of the audience to which his art is addressed. The classics are classics because accumulated experience has found in them the most permanently satisfying embodiment of values that have gained universal assent. The stature of Beethoven was not measurable either by himself or by his contemporaries. Unnumbered music lovers have magnified his art by comprehending it and, from among many prophets, have declared him to be true. So, it is to be hoped, will posterity deal with us, seeing clearly where we have failed or where succeeded in the cultivation of new and fertile expedients, and on our children will also fall the responsibility of choosing from among us those creative artists who, in the accepted medium, had things of greatest import to say. We may envy our successors their perspective. We cannot forestall their verdict.

INDEX OF COMPOSERS

B

INDEX OF COMPOSERS

150

INDEX OF COMPOSERS

INDEX OF COMPOSERS